Share Your Testimony

Volume 1:

Women Who Overcome

Share Your Testimony Volume 1: Women Who Overcome
Copyright © 2017 by Rhonda Dickerson, Elise B. Gordon, Leslie Foxx, Taneya Pair, Desiree G. Smith, and Shanice L. Stewart

Printed in the United States of America.

ISBN-13: 978-0692919422 Printed Version

Edited by: Red Ink Editing

RedInkEditing2017@gmail.com

Book Cover Designed By: Branded 1428

info@branded1428.com

Follow us on Instagram: Share_Your_Testimony15

Like us on Facebook: Share Your Testimony15

Dedication

This book is dedicated to you. To the one who needs a push to continue your journey. To the one who feels like giving up right in the middle of your process. To the one who needs encouragement to breakthrough and move forward in your purpose. This book is dedicated to the one who believes in the word overcome and receives it as their portion for his/her life. This book is for you, to uplift your spirit and to remind you that you are not alone. This book was written to remind you that even though you messed up in life, God can still use you for His glory. This book is to remind you that there is nothing that you can do that will ever separate you from the love of God. As you take your leap of faith, lean and depend on what God has shown and told you. As you follow the direction of Holy Spirit who leads and directs you daily, you will overcome and your testimony will transform and impact many lives. We love you and God loves you even more. As willing vessels, we yield to what God desires to do throughout the testimonies in this book. God has dedicated this book to you and your destiny. God has dedicated this book to you, to remind you that you are chosen and beautiful in His eyes (spiritually, physically, and emotionally). You are a blessing to God and His gift to the world.

With love,

Taneya Pair

Table of Contents

Introduction...6

Leslie Foxx...8

Desiree G. Smith...20

Elise B. Gordon..38

Rhonda Dickerson...52

Shanice L. Stewart...68

Taneya Pair..84

About the Authors..104

Introduction

In August 2015, I went on with my day like any other day, until God to release a vision in my spirit that would shift my entire life. God gave me clear instructions, "I want you to have an event called *Share Your Testimony*, where women will come and share their testimonies". I was so excited! I said, "Ok God, let's do it!"

By the time September rolled around, reality set in. Reality a.k.a. Fear. I thought to myself, how in the world am I going to make this event happen. I prayed for God to bless me with a team, because I knew I could not bring this vision to manifestation by myself. God answered that prayer. He blessed me with the incredible women who's powerful testimonies you are about to read. I will cherish their support, sacrifice, love, and prayers forever! Not only did they believe in the vision that God gave me, but they grabbed hold of the vision and helped bring it to manifestation. When God gives you a vision, please know He has already made provision. All you have to do is walk in faith, knowing God will be with you every step of the way. In other words, ***All you have to do is trust God and jump!***

When we share God's goodness and mercy, we defeat the enemy because he desires for us to walk in fear and not in faith, to live life purposeless and not purposeful, and to stay in spiritual bondage and not walk in total freedom. This book was written to encourage you that God loves you unconditionally and He will never turn His back on you.

In 2016, we hosted five amazing *Share Your Testimony* Events. These events have been powerful and iife changing! Women have connected with other women. I have witnessed women receive their healing through the testimonies of other women. I have also witnessed women receive their healing of their past by sharing their own testimony! We give God ALL the glory for this incredible vision.

Share Your Testimony is a women's ministry to encourage, inspire, and strengthen women through the testimonies of other women.

Months after we launched *Share Your Testimony*, I asked God what's next. He said, "Turn *Share Your Testimony* into a series of books." I was totally blown away! God is so faithful over His promises towards us. I just want to remind you that whatever God has promised you, it's going to come to pass. Don't allow the spirit of fear to stop you from fulfilling your purpose. Just trust God and jump!

It's my prayer that these powerful testimonies in this book will bless, encourage, inspire, strengthen, and motivate you. These ladies definitely don't look like what they have been through. They are truly Overcomers! And you are too!

Shanice L. Stewart

Share Your Testimony, Visionary

Leslie Foxx

"Thou art my hiding place and my shield; I hope in thy Word." Psalm 119:114

I am incredibly honored to share my story. I fought with myself spiritually to never open that part of life ever again. The reason being is, "Fear". I feared the criticism and backlash from people who would look at me differently. The enemy will have you believe that your story will not empower people. I chose to step out of fear, because someone needs to hear my story. Someone is waiting on me to share my testimony. God delivered me from it; now it's time to tell it. God preserved me for this purpose. He preserved me even through my mess ups. If telling my story can help another sister or brother, then to God be the glory. If my story causes judgment from others, well to God be the glory anyhow. God bless the reader through the reading of this book. I pray that even now God will start at the root of what needs to be plucked out of you. Amen!

What exactly in life have you revisited in your mind? We constantly can relive our past with present events that seem familiar. For example, abusive relationships, bitterness, drama, low self-esteem, and failures. In order to deal with the mind and how it operates, you have to get to the root of it. When did it start? Where did it come from? Some roots that are planted can be generational curses. Generational curses are seeds of sin that are planted and grow from generation to generation. Some of the barriers we deal with are seeds. What seed did Adam and Eve plant for the generations after them? Not even knowing exactly what seed could have been planted from your mom or dad. Are you repeating the same habits of your parents? What areas of your life seem to stand out the most? The area that stands out the most in my life came from my childhood.

My life involved being three different people; from three different angles. I was Leslie Robinson, Leslie Williams, and I am now Leslie Foxx. Growing up as Leslie Robinson, I am the youngest of my two sisters. I lived with my grandparents, mom, and sisters. I have the darkest complexion out of both of my sisters.

One of my aunts used to treat me quite different than my sisters. I never understood why she never liked me. She attacked my complexion a lot, so I figured it had a lot to do with me not being light enough to fit into her "like only zone". The root to my low self-esteem came from this part of my life. I was called monkey, black ape, dirty, and whatever else she could think of. I went through this for many years.

In my eyes, my grandparents had the most perfect marriage. I admired how they stuck by each other's side through thick and thin. Grandma was a woman after God's own heart; a powerful praying woman. When she prayed, she left a residue in the room that would make you shout! I wanted a marriage like hers. I wanted a prayer life like hers. It's funny when we see a perfect vase, we only see the beauty of it. We don't see how the potter put the clay together. We view the most admirable relationships the same way. Sometimes we see the "perfect" marriage and say, "I want what they have". Are you truly ready to experience what they went through to get what they have? It takes going through the pressing, shaking, and down moments. Even when the areas in your marriage begin to get tough: Are you willing to stand on God's Word concerning your marriage? Every Saturday night, my grandmother would gather the family together for Saturday night prayer. All of us even down to the grandchildren were on our knees crying out to the Lord. I didn't have the strength to pray as long as everyone else, so I would fall asleep right where I was kneeling. Sometimes I wondered if that was a way to get all the grandkids asleep. Grandma held the family together.

I remember one day she said, "Somebody is going to have a lot of kids". I was about 10 or 11 years old when she said it. Even as a child, I carried a lot of emotional baggage. I truly believed I was the ugliest child ever born. When I finally heard that I was beautiful from a man's mouth, I fell for him. I just knew that this man wanted to be with me. If not, would he have really said I was beautiful? I figured here goes my perfect marriage like my grandparents. At the age of 12, I gave my virginity away to a 22 year old man. I slept with him on numerous occasions. I figured giving myself to him would allow a door to be opened for love and acceptance. Instead, I opened a door for more spirits. We don't realize when you lay down with different men and allow them to enter you; you are also allowing different spirits to live in you as well. This is called a "Soul Tie", which opened up a door for promiscuous behavior. These are seeds that were planted: rejection, depression, low self-esteem, anger, and promiscuous behavior. The seeds that take root in us, can also take root in our children. This is an example of the repeated pattern of generational curses.

I became pregnant at the age of 15, and delivered my daughter at the age of 16. I moved in with my daughter's father, because I was still yet trying to find my perfect life. I did manage to stay in school. My mother and I relationship was not the best, because I had truly disappointed her with the decisions that I made. She had high expectations of me, but I allowed my feelings to become a wall. Sometimes we take our parents discipline as a way of them trying to stop our lives, but we don't realize that they are trying to steer us in the right direction. I didn't want to follow my mom's directions. I wanted to follow my own. I felt pain the day I told my grandmother I no longer wanted to live in her house. Her words were, "Let her go, she has to learn just like everyone else". I truly thought I was making grown-up decisions.

Everything was going well in the beginning when I first moved out. After a while, things took a complete turn. I started receiving what I didn't expect. Sometimes things became physical between my boyfriend and me. I remember the time when I had a swollen jaw, and that very next day my grandmother called because she had seen what happened in a vision. She described the whole episode to me, and wasn't even physically there. She kept warning me to return home before I ended up dead. I truly believe it was my grandmother's prayers that covered and protected me. The more people tried to keep me away from my boyfriend, the more I wanted to be with him. Our relationship became a strong soul tie. Anything he wanted me to do, I did it. We had a love hate relationship. There were days that we loved each other and other days we hated each other. It seemed like the only time we could communicate with one another was through sexual intercourse.

I eventually had two kids while in high school, and when I graduated, I was pregnant with my third. The sad part was I did not attend my own high school graduation, because I wanted to attend his graduation to see the female that he was messing around on me with. I thought being at his graduation was more important than being at mines. I received a scholarship for college, but I ended up dropping out because I was chasing behind "love". I felt like I started turning into his mother, because I looked forward to changing him and making him the way that I desired; instead of him making the clear decision of changing himself. I learned that when a man's heart is aligned up with God's Word, his change will come through the Word of God and not forced. Let me explain what I mean. A woman should not have to force a man to love her. When he desires to please God first, he has already made a choice to love you, especially when he doesn't want to disappoint God. I made a lot of reckless decisions by chasing who and what I wanted to be my forever.

Eventually, I started hearing even less from my grandmother, than what I normally would. We always expect for our grandparents to live forever. In my mind, my grandmother was doing fine. The last time I talked to her, I remember her saying, "I will be there when you have that baby". On one particular day, I was at the bus station waiting for my bus to arrive, I ran into one of my friends I knew from elementary school. She went into a deep conversation about a funeral she attended three months ago. In the middle of the conversation she said, "Leslie, I went to your grandmother's funeral". That's the only thing I heard clear. I felt my heart beating hard and the baby in my womb jumping. I shouted at her, "Please stop lying!" I remember running home, I could not even wait for the bus. I literally ran home, which was about seven blocks away. When I arrived home, I immediately ran to the phone to call my grandmother. I just knew she would answer. The phone kept ringing, so I kept hanging up and calling right back. No answer! I imagined that she was going to pick up that phone on the other end, and everything was going to be a lie. So I kept calling. I fell to my knees in tears. My grandmother been gone for three months; FOR THREE MONTHS and nobody told me! Did my family hate me that much? Were they ashamed of me that much? I was hurt and heartbroken. That pain was indescribable. When you are constantly being hurt, it begins to break you down mentally and physically. At this point in my life, I started feeling rejection. I was tired of the hurt and pain. At this point I no longer wanted to be bothered with my family. I felt as though since I was the black sheep in the family, then I needed to just keep my distance.

My living situation was not the best, but I had to make due with what we had. I held onto a lot of what my grandmother taught me. She instilled in me a great foundation and it was truly time to put those instructions into action. One thing that she said was, "You can do whatever you set your mind to do. If you don't do the work, you don't get the results". I was determined to get out of my living condition. I remember long nights of water and electric turned off in the middle of winter. I remember nights of waking up to the smell of a burning metal pipe and thick smoke in the air. If you don't know what that is, it's the smell of crack cocaine being burned in a pipe with brass. It's a very sickening smell that made me nauseous. The person that we were living with had a drug addiction. You always knew when they were high, because they became very paranoid as if someone was chasing them through the house. I went through moments of them leaving their children behind for weeks, and I had to take care of their kids along with my own. I knew at this point the only one that could get me out of this situation was God. I had been raised in church all of my life. Of course the things of the world became very tempting to me. That's how the enemy presents himself. I knew of God, but I did not have a relationship with Him. I tried living off my grandmother and mother's residue of prayer. When I no longer had that access available, God had to put me in a place where I had to find Him for myself. One thing I never forgot was, if it worked for my grandmother, then I know it has to work for me too. I kept trying to hold onto what God wanted me to let go of. Sometimes what you think is yours, really does not belong to you. That's why the word of God says, "What therefore God hath joined together, let not man put asunder" (Mark 10:9). Many relationships we find ourselves in are not ordained by God. Even the enemy can send a decoy that looks attractive.

Even as I write and look back over my life, I have truly put myself in situations that God was calling me out of. I wanted what I wanted. I wanted love. The love that I was trying so hard to chase was not the love God had for me. In reality, it wasn't love at all. Incredibly, God's grace over my life was a sign of unconditional love. So many nights I could have been killed for being in harms way, but God preserved me. I was living in a house with different men and women entering and leaving throughout the night doing drugs. I had to chase people out, because they were getting high while the children were in the house. I had items stolen from me and sold for drug purchases. I literally was tired of going through this.

In 2004, I married at the age of 18 and tried to live out the life my grandmother had. It felt like a battle. My marriage lasted for seven years. That last year of my marriage was critical. In 2005, God opened up a door for me and my family to leave. By this time

14

I had five children, which included one set of twins that were born at 25 weeks. The same babies that the doctor declared would not live, are now 11 years old. Nothing but God!

In May 2009, I experienced a day of turmoil. It was a day that caused me to lose my mind. My husband ran the bath water for our five year old son. My husband didn't realize how hot the water was and put our son in the tub. The skin on my son's feet turned into puss bubbles. I immediately took my son to the emergency room. We weren't at the hospital long before Social Services were called. When you are living in a society as a young person, making low income, and have a lot of children, you fit into the ratio of being an abusive and neglectful parent. We couldn't afford a lawyer or anything and everything was court appointed.

By this time, we had seven children and our youngest baby was only ten months old. The very next day the social worker called me to come back up to the hospital to bring my other children for an examination. I did what was asked, because I had nothing to hide because what happened to my son was an accident. The social worker assured me that she just wanted to see them. When I arrived at the hospital, there were five police officers there. I had never been through this situation before and I didn't have an understanding of what was going on. They took all my children. Even as I am writing this, I feel myself tearing up! The social worker walked up to me with three of those officers and snatched my baby right out of my hands. It felt like my soul left my body. I fell to the floor in tears, as I heard the screams and cries of my children being pulled down the hallway, until I could no longer hear the sound of their voices anymore. The last voice I heard was my youngest baby, who was crying for me.

That same night, the social worker called my phone to torment me. She allowed me to hear my baby crying, so that she could get what she needed from us. They typed up a paper full of lies, and wanted my husband and I to sign it. The first thing they said was, "If you don't sign it, you will never see your kids again!" For five long years, I fought for my children to return home. It was hard because I was receiving low income and didn't have the proper help to get the law on my side. This situation pulled my husband and I further apart. I started throwing hard blows at him verbally, because I felt like he wasn't emotional enough that our children were gone. I did not know how to handle it. I started drinking heavy. Alcohol became my pillow. All I wanted was to get my kids home.

After I had my seventh child, I had my tubes tied. I knew my husband was upset about my decision. He wanted more children, but I was completely done at this point. I was mad at God and everything else. I wondered why He allowed something like this to happen to me. My children were sexually and physically abused while in foster care. I felt like I was powerless as a mother, because I couldn't save them. I couldn't get to them. I knew they cried out for me, but I wasn't there to rescue them. At this point, I was mentally messed up. When I found out my husband had a baby on the way in the middle of us fighting to get our children home, I was so angry! I questioned God. How is it that my children were taken away, and You allowed him to have another child? Why must I suffer? God had to remind me that I stepped out on my marriage too! His sin was not greater than mine.

By me being so judgmental, I ended up sleeping with a married man. There is nothing to justify being married or separated and sleeping with someone outside of your marriage. Those negative emotions and feelings that we build up are not of God, and I built up a lot of it. We had too many mouths on our marriage, wrong company, and most importantly, God was not in it. When you have the wrong company around your marriage, it can tear it down. By me not having a relationship with God, the enemy had me blind to what was really happening in my life. It is very important to have discernment of the people in your circle.

Once we started sleeping with other people, it allowed transferring of spirits. I even started desiring women, to a point where I no longer wanted to be with a man. Through the cleansing of the blood of Jesus Christ; everything shifted and changed for me, but I had to surrender. I had to surrender my life to God and realize I needed God. Sometimes we forget that God is a forgiven God. It was God through the blood of Jesus Christ that cleansed me. I rededicated my life to Christ and moved in a different direction. Everything that I had lost was returned back to me; my children, marriage, a home and job. God has been so good to me that I can go on and on. God is even using the lives of my children to empower other people through their testimonies. Even in my marriage now, God is our foundation. God has blessed me with a great man who loves God, me, and all seven of my children.

Even in my marriage now, I am so amazed. This marriage is so different than my last marriage. To have a man who literally speaks in my life spiritually, who prays and covers me. Who seeks the face of God and runs after His heart. Who encourages me and supports my visions. Who studies his word daily and loves my children as his own. It was difficult when my sons first came home from the foster system, because they were hurt and broken. I can't teach my sons how to be men, I can only give them knowledge from a woman's perspective. I was scared to open the door for any man to come into our lives, because I felt like I had to protect my children. I wanted to be their shield.

After all of the scars from what they endured, I wanted to prevent them from being hurt again. The problem with this was I began to build a wall from everyone. Now, if I would have kept that door closed pushing purpose out of my children would have been complicated. I thank God that I decided to open that door. If I would have kept that door closed, I can't even imagine exactly what the circumstance would be. Sometimes we shut doors in our lives, because we are afraid to open them because of our past pain. My children and I were all emotional; too many emotional beings will eventually collapse. God sent my husband to keep us from collapsing.

God had to change my name. I am now Leslie Foxx, married to Maurice Foxx and I thank God for him. Sometimes all I can do is just stare at him. I still smile when I look back at our wedding pictures. Your husband should be able to feed you spiritually and minister to you; and not just around for natural pleasure. Your first ministry is home.

It took for me to go through all of this to realize what my purpose was. Don't let the enemy fill your mind with lies. He will use your past against you, but God has already raised up a standard against him. What you were, is not who you are. God's plans are bigger than our plans. Just surrender and allow God to reveal Himself in your life. There are so many stories I would love to share concerning my life, however, God used me to share this part of my journey with you. God bless the reader, and prayerfully my testimony has been a blessing.

Desiree G. Smith

"Yea, though I walk through the valley of the shadow of death, I will fear no evil: for thou art with me; thy rod and thy staff they comfort me." Psalm 23:4

As I sit here writing my testimony, I give all the glory and honor to Jesus Christ. He is the only one that gives me grace and mercy. It's funny, as a kid we all dream of what we would become as adults. During the course of my life, I had so many plans that were not aligned with God's plan and purpose for my life. During my second layoff in 2014 and through the healing process of writing, God birthed me with the passion to help heal others by sharing my experiences. I can recall staying up late writing my testimonies down on paper. God altered my dream so that I can fulfill His purpose and plan for my life.

"For I know the plans I have for you, declares the Lord, plans to prosper you and not to harm you plans to give you hope and a future." Jeremiah 29:11

Throughout my life I have been physically, emotionally, and mentally abused. I grew up in a home without indoor plumbing or a bathroom. My own father denied me. Here is my testimony.

Let this testimony be the Sunshine to your Hope, Future, and Destiny.

Life without being Daddy's Little Princess

The last memory as a child that I have of my dad was during my early childhood, I was around the age of five and it was springtime. My dad picked me up from my grandma's house and took me to The Cross Road Store. He brought me some penny candy about 100 pieces which was only a dollar, but to me it was a million dollars. At that moment, I was living my dream of being daddy's little princess. That was the last time I ever felt that way. As the days, weeks, and months went by, I didn't see or hear from my dad. I asked my mom, "Where's my daddy?" She replied, "I don't know". I then realized that my father wasn't coming back for me. My heart was beyond broken, I wanted to be daddy's little girl. At five I was empty, confused, lost, and looking for approval from a male. I learned at five that man will disappoint you every time. I can recall wondering why other children had their fathers and I didn't. What did I do so bad to make my father leave me? I always knew in my heart that one day my dad was coming back for me.

I remember visiting my grandmother (dad's mom) on several occasions. She lived in a brick home with three bedrooms and a basement. My grandma had a flower garden in her basement. As time went on, I remember thinking to myself "Why do I have to live poorly?" My grandma has a house that is big enough for me to live in and I wouldn't have to be put in so much danger every day. I feared for me and my family's lives every day. The house that I grew up in was a little house that was built around the late 40's by my grandfather. He built the house himself; it was a four-room house with no plumbing in the kitchen and no bathroom. The house only had a kitchen, two bedrooms, and a living room. The toilet was a bucket or out house, the tub was a round silver tub, and two pails were used to wash dishes and/or hands. There was no heating or cooling system in the house. We used fans in the summer and a wood stove in the winter. While the house was built in the 40's, the only update to our home was electricity. It was never updated with much else.

The house was built at a time when most blacks didn't own a home or land, my grandfather did both. However, by the time I was born in the late 70's things had changed and homes were built with plumbing, electricity, heating and cooling systems. My dad and grandmother lived in nice houses compared to the house I was living in. My life wasn't fair and I knew at a very young age what it was like to be abused, neglected, and poor. I was given the worse opportunity to succeed at life. The odds were stacked against me. How was I going to survive? I wanted to live in a house and have the basic things like a bathroom and plumbing. Many days and nights I cried out for my father and I wanted to live with him. At the age of eight, I was sexually abused by a family member. My innocence was stolen from me. For many years I believed that it was all my fault, because my father didn't want or love me anymore. I hated my father for letting me live under those circumstances.

I went on to live the next few years of my life without my dad. I continued to long for my father and seek approval from males. I would talk about my dad to my friends. I would make up stories about him. I told lies about him visiting me on the weekend or him buying me stuff. I talked about how great a father he was and how we would go shopping for new shoes. I was often embarrassed at school, because I had to wear whatever brand of shoes that my mother could afford. My dad wasn't helping my mother at all; he never sent her any money to cover my expenses. She was doing the best that she could to make ends meet to provide for me.

When 1987 rolled around and my sister was born, things changed for us. Money was even tighter, and I received even less things because the baby needed more than I did. My mom only made minimum wage. My mom, sister, and I needed personal items, clothes, food and shoes. My mom signed up for assistance and the WIC program to receive help with the baby's milk and other items like bread and peanut butter. All I knew was that we were poor and it was my dad's fault. I was teased at school, because of my clothes, shoes, and the car we drove.

Court Day

I was about 13 years old when my mom finally took my dad to court for child support. When we arrived at the courthouse, I was nervous because I hadn't seen or heard from my dad since I was about five years old. A part of me was happy because now just maybe I can be his little princess again like I use to be. During this court hearing, I heard the most hurtful words a girl could ever hear from her father. My dad told the Judge, "She isn't my daughter". My world came crashing down once again. Now I knew the truth, I wasn't ever going to be his little princess. My whole life was destroyed and my heart was broken into many pieces. I never wanted to see him again. At that moment, I knew what a thin line between love and hate truly meant. Thoughts began racing through my head: "Why is this happening to me? Dad, you don't love me anymore? Why are you saying this? Why don't you want to give us any money?"

The Judge ordered DNA testing before child support could be rendered. After a couple of weeks, we went back to court for the DNA test results. The results are in YOU ARE THE FATHER!!!!!!!!! The judge ordered my father to pay child support and carry medical and dental insurance (I never had medical or dental insurance even after the order). After all assessments of income and expenses, my father was ordered to pay $120 a month until I turned 18 or graduated from high school. I knew that it cost more than that to buy shoes, clothes, and food each month. My mom and I only received $120 a month, but it was better than nothing, which we had for the previous 13 years. My dad only had to help take care of me for the last five years of my entire life. All I was to him was an extra bill he had to pay. After that day in court, I never saw my dad. I longed for the day that I could have dinner and long conversations with him.

A father is supposed to be the first male cheerleader in a young girl's life. As for me, I didn't experience those life moments with my father. He never attended a track meet, band concert, choir recital, graduation, or school program; he simply walked out of my life. My grandma would always talk with his mother frequently. I only had seen my dad's mom a few times after that as well. However, my grandma always managed to talk with her. As much as I needed my dad during my critical teenage years, I didn't have him. The only thing I had was $120 a month that I would fight and argue my mother for, because I felt it was to support me.

During high school, I had carried much of the burden from my early childhood into my teenage years. *(Psalm 55:22 "Cast thy burden upon the Lord, and he shall sustain thee: he shall never suffer the righteous to be moved." KJV)* I fought and argued with my mother on many occasions about different things. I was angry at her, my father, and the world. My mother and I didn't have the best relationship. I always had an understanding of God, because I went to church every Sunday and choir rehearsal during the week. My relationship with God wasn't present at this time in my life. Honestly, at times I doubted God. I thought if God was real, why wasn't He saving me?

My graduation day was in June 1995. I was so happy to finally graduate from high school and finally getting away my life. I graduated from high school and my father wasn't there. I was very disappointed that he didn't show up on one of the most important days of my life. As I prepared to go off to college that summer, my father wasn't there for me at all. In fact, I didn't even tell him that I was going to college my grandma did.

College Days

I got accepted into a small HBCU, Saint Paul's College (SPC). I chose SPC because they were offering me the most financial aid at the time. In August 1995, my family dropped me off at SPC with $200. I was truly scared and all I had was $200. I managed to make some new friends and began to fit into this new world of mine. Like many other college students, I began to drink and party. The drinking at times helped me to ease the pain of my childhood. There were times I would drink so much that I didn't know what happened or I started some trouble with someone.

I can recall one semester not having enough money for books, so I contacted my father and told him that I needed $200 for books. He told me that he didn't have it and if he did, he wasn't going to give it me. He proceeded to tell me that if I need money I needed to contact my mother not him, because he wasn't going to help me. I hung the phone up on him and proceeded to write (no email at the time) him a letter. In the letter, I told him that I was no longer his child. I proceeded to write to him that he would never meet his grandchildren and that he wouldn't walk me down the aisle when I get married. He never wrote me back nor spoke with me during my four years at SPC. I continued to drink and party during my entire time at SPC. I ended up in reckless situations with guys at the school. I never had a boyfriend during college, just a couple "friends" with benefits. There were times in college when I really needed that $120 a month that my mom was receiving for child support. I needed money for books, food, clothes, shoes, and toiletries.

During my freshman year in college, I decided to go and try out for the track team. At first I didn't want to run track, because I was wore out from running in middle and high school. I made the track team and earned a partial track scholarship to help cover my tuition in addition to many other scholarships. No matter the circumstances, I was determined to finish and get my degree. It was God's grace and mercy that I made it through and graduated with my degree. My grandma would send me money and care packages. My mom would send money when she could. I mainly relied on God's grace and mercy.

I graduated in May 1999 with my Bachelor's Degree in Criminal Justice. I remember a few days prior to graduation, my grandma called to tell me that my dad's mom had passed away from cancer. Even though I didn't have a relationship with her like my grandma, I cried and was saddened by her death. I recall walking across that stage and my family was there except my father. I returned home after graduation and went to my grandma's funeral. My grandmother and I sat in the back; I didn't want to be acknowledged. My father and great aunt saw me at the funeral. A few days after the funeral, my father asked me to meet him at the bank. When I arrived at the bank, he handed me an envelope with $200 and told me that he was proud of me for graduating college and apologized to me. God will mend a broken relationship.

Building the Bridges

After the day my father apologized to me, we began to build our relationship. We would talk occasionally and I would go visit him at his home. I recall one day while I was visiting him at his home, I saw a picture of this young lady who favored my dad. I asked him who the girl was. He told me no one. The girl in the picture stayed in my mind for a long time. This was also during the time that my grandma (mother's mom) was diagnosed with stage four cancer. Her health was declining fast. She fought her battle with cancer for about 18 months and lost it in February 2001. I grieved my grandmother's death for a long time.

During the spring of that year, I relocated to the Washington D.C. area. I kept in contact with my father. He didn't think that it was a good idea that I moved to the area, but I did it anyway. He would talk to me about the traffic and accidents that occurred in the area. In November 2002, my mom and family from Connecticut met me in Maryland for Thanksgiving. I received a call from my aunt who told me that I needed to come home because my father was in hospital in Winston-Salem, NC. The next day I packed up and took my mother home. I picked up my aunt who rode with me to the hospital to see my father. He was in the ICU unit at the hospital and only immediate family could see him. I remember when the doctor came out and said "The Johnson Family". I stood up and so did this other young lady. We both walked up to the doctor and were escorted back to his room. We both asked, "Who are you?" We both replied, "I am his daughter". We both stood there looking at our father with tubes down his mouth. That was the first time I had met one of my sisters. My sister got on the phone and called my other sister. We arranged to meet for dinner later that night.

A few days later, my father was released from the hospital. My sisters and I began to ask him why didn't he get us all together and tell us about each other. We all began to communicate with one another over the next few months. I learned that I was an Auntie at the time; I had two nephews and one niece. During the summer of 2003, my mom was at work when she overheard a young lady talking about her father. My mother asked her who her father was, it turns out she was the young lady in the picture that I had asked my father about. As time went on, I continued to build my relationship with my father and three sisters. In addition to the three sisters that I had met and talked to, I also had my baby sister who lived out of state. In December 2003, my father was scheduled to have surgery. Unfortunately, he didn't make it to have the surgery, he passed away.

I am so grateful that we were able to build our relationship. God had ordained the healing of our relationship. Although we didn't get a chance to have a family dinner prior to my father's death, I thank God for the time that I did get to spend with him.

The Road to Having My First Child

This part of my story reminds me of Sarah in Bible.

Genesis 17:16-17 "I will bless her and will surely give you a son by her. I will bless her so that she will be the mother of nations; kings of peoples will come from her. Abraham fell facedown; he laughed and said to himself, will a son be born to a man hundred years old? Will Sarah bear a child at the age of ninety?"

Genesis 21:1 "Now the Lord was gracious to Sarah as he had said, and the Lord did what he has promised." (NIV)

Has anyone ever said these hurtful, harmful, or spiteful words to you?

- I guess your mama/daddy will only have one grandchild or no grandchildren.
- Looks like you are never going to have kids.
- Oh my God you are 30 and you don't have any kids.
- When are you going to have a baby?
- Can you even have a baby?
- What are you waiting for? Your eggs are going to dry up.
- When are you going to have a grandchild for me?
- Maybe you should adopt a child; there are plenty of kids who need a home.

These are all the things that have been said to me for many years of my life. These words came from family, friends, lovers, and neighbors. All of these negatives comments were hurtful to me. The truth is sometimes I would tell people: I don't want any kids, I can't afford kids, and are you going to take care of them for me? Deep down inside, I knew that I always wanted to be a mother someday. I wanted to be the best mother I could be and give my child(ren) the opportunities that I didn't have growing up. I always thought in the back of my mind that I was incapable of having children, because of the physical abuse I endured. I spent many days and nights worrying about not being able to have children. I thought I was incapable of having kids based on stories I have been told and what I seen on the show *Law & Order*.

One day I was having pain in my side so bad that I went to the emergency room. I was examined and told to go see an

29

OB/GYN immediately, because there was a mass on my ovaries. I didn't have an OB/GYN, because I had only been in MD for a year. In a hurry, I searched and found a doctor that I chose as my doctor primarily because she had my last name. This is called faith. I called the office and was able to get an appointment real fast. My doctor told me that I needed surgery right away, like the next day or within the week. I had a cyst on my ovaries the size of a grapefruit and if it wasn't removed it could burst. If it bursts then I may be at risk for not being able to have a child in the future. I talked with the doctor to explain to her that I can't have a surgery right away, because I needed at least a month to get all of my finances in order. She granted me the month, but warned me of all the potential dangers and risks. I got things in order the best I could and left the rest up to God.

In September 2003, I had surgery on my ovary to remove the cyst. Prior to surgery, my doctor explained to me that potentially I could have a partial or full hysterectomy depending on what she finds. As I awoke from the surgery, my first question to her was: Can I still have kids? She replied "yes". I was so happy! I had defeated the devil and his distraction, and through Christ I had won this battle.

Post-Surgery Testimony:

In the midst of all of this, I had just moved into my apartment. On my job the only benefit I had was health insurance. I didn't receive leave, dental insurance, retirement, vacation or sick leave not even short and long term disability. I had to go on leave without pay during my recovery. My recovery period for my surgery was 4-6 weeks. I wasn't sure how long it was going to take for my recovery. I was blessed to have a four week recovery period. God truly showed me favor. When I left for my surgery, I had $800 in my account. I was able to pay my bills and have food on the table. However, when I returned to work I had to work a month *before I got paid. I was out of cash and I only had enough money to pay rent. On my first day back to work, my co-workers had collected over $500 for me.*

Fast forward three years later; I went to get my routine pap smear. This one pap smear test came back abnormal. All kinds of thoughts went rushing through my head. I started to think that I had cancer, I am going to die young, I don't have any kids, this can't be happening to me. The doctor found pre-cancerous cells on my cervix. The good news is it was 100% curable. Thank you Jesus!!!!! I had a procedure done to freeze the cells on my cervix. The procedure only took about 30-45 minutes in the office. I could return to work the next day. It's only by God's grace and mercy that I was saved and didn't have cancer. God had ordained this; He led me to my doctor to save my life twice. Over the next two to three years, I had abnormal pap smears, which resulted in having a pap smear done every six months. After I received the news of a normal pap smear, I continued to have a pap smear done every six months for the next year.

During this test, I had to endure people saying all those hurtful and thoughtless comments about me like, "When are you going to have kids? Don't you want kids?" During a time of bereavement, one person said to me: "Well, I guess your mama won't get any grandbabies from you. Aren't you getting too old to have a baby? I guess she better enjoy the one she has." (See at this time in my life, I had a better relationship with my Heavenly Father.) I responded, "It isn't over yet, God will bless me with a child. Don't count me out." My flesh wanted to slap that lady. She didn't have a clue what she was saying to me, nor did she know my situation and she definitely wasn't God. She was just a vessel the devil used at that moment to test me.

I was praying and waiting. I knew one thing, I wasn't going to have a baby with someone who didn't want a baby, just to say that I have a child. I didn't want to struggle to raise a child either. I struggled all of my childhood and most of my adult life. I came very close to having a hysterectomy and cancer. I wasn't supposed to be alive today, but God stepped in and canceled premature death from my life. The devil had me bound with lies, diseases, molestation, fatherlessness, and hopelessness. I had to relinquish those things that had me bound. If you want to receive what God has for you, you will need to relinquish some things in your life too. He doesn't want to bless you, and then you mistreat or misuse the blessing He has given to you. *(James 4:7 "Submit yourselves therefore to God. Resist the devil, and he will flee from you." KJV)*

On a beautiful day in April 2012, I can recall not getting my cycle. I thought to myself, I am a pregnant! I was happy and scared all at the same time. I was scared because my fiancé and I hadn't even been dating a year. I wasn't sure what our future was going to be at the time. I was happy because I was finally receiving a blessing of a child from God. I was 35 at the time, which in today's medical standard is advance maternal age. My due date came, but no baby. My doctor said that if the baby doesn't come within the next week, then they will induce my labor.

I went to my last doctor's visit and was instructed to go have a sonogram done. During the sonogram, they discovered that the ammonic fluid surrounding the baby was low. I was instructed to go straight to the hospital. I was so nervous, because I knew that my baby was in danger. I said a quick prayer, "Lord, please let my baby be ok". We went straight to the hospital. We didn't have breakfast or any bags with us. We didn't even have the car seat installed in the car. The doctor began to induce my labor. Over the next few hours labor didn't progress, my cervix never dilated nor did my water break. During labor induction, the doctor couldn't find the baby's heartbeat. The labor induction was stopped and I was monitored throughout the night. My labor didn't progress with any of the procedures. My cervix wasn't going to thin out due to the previous procedure I had done. We had to make the decision the next day on what would be best for the baby. The next day my son was born healthy via C-section.

Seeking Career and Purpose

God's grace and mercy continues to reign over my life regarding my career, purpose, and passion. During the course of my working years, I have grown from unhappiness, underemployed, and unemployed.

During my elementary school years, I managed to earn good grades. Once I entered the 6th grade, things changed because the real work began and play time ended. This was scary to me, but I started to think about what I wanted to become when I became an adult, because time was moving fast. I was fascinated with the law. I wanted to help people and put away people who harmed others. I loved the way that they dressed in suits and stated their cases. My goal was to become an attorney and own my own law firm. I spent my whole entire middle and high school years focusing on becoming a lawyer.

In the 12th grade we had the opportunity to go on a career day assignment. My assignment was the courthouse. I was so excited, because this was my first time ever going to a courthouse to hear a criminal case. After the assignment, I was ready for college and selected Criminal Justice as my major. After declaring my major, I received some disturbing news from the school guidance counselor. She explained to me that I would not be able to attend a four-year college or university. I was devastated beyond measure, because I knew that there was nothing more that I wanted for my life more than becoming a lawyer. Despite what I was told, I did attend a four-year college and received my B.A. in Criminal Justice. After graduation, it took me a few months to land a job. I landed a job as a Correctional Officer at the Caswell Correctional Facility. I worked there for 11 months before leaving the position. I worked in a group home for a while, this job was awesome and the schedule was good.

Soon after, I relocated to the DMV area hoping for better career opportunities. Prior to moving, I landed a job in a group home. I was hired as a Case Manager; I applied to job after job in the state, local, and federal governments. I finally landed a job as a Case Manager for the Department of Corrections (DOC). I worked at this job for six years and I performed three job functions. I gained a lot of knowledge and experience from working there, but it still wasn't enough; I wanted more. While I was working there, I went back to school and pursued my Master's Degree in Public Administration.

When I finally left the DOC, I went into federal government contracting. I experienced my first ever layoff in June 2009. Like always, God carried me through this difficult time. I was able to maintain all my bills. I was also able to keep my apartment and car (which I had just brought the year before). I had to lean on God like never before. It took me about five months to return to the work force. I finally landed a job as a helpdesk specialist, which I had no training or knowledge to complete the work.

After two years of working on the Helpdesk, I moved onto another contracting job. Shortly after I returned from Maternity leave in March, I was told that the contract would not be renewed, and once again I was facing unemployment. Unemployment wasn't an option, because I just had a baby and brought a home. I received a call to become the Manager at my old job. I took the opportunity, but I was a little hesitant because I knew the people and sometimes that's not always a great position to be in. I worked as the Manager for a little over a year. It had its challenges, but the experience was great.

I knew that once I accepted the position that it was only for year, but I still took on the challenge. The contract was up in June and I was yet again facing unemployment. My company found a place for me for the next four months. My assignment ended in November. I was offered a job in December. When I started working on my first day, the client asked that all personnel be interviewed again through him. At the end of the process, I wasn't selected for position. During this time of unemployment, some days I found myself in a depressed mood. I didn't understand why I wasn't hearing anything back from the jobs I applied to. I applied for so many positions during my eight months of unemployment.

During my time of unemployment in 2014-2015, I began to journal. Here are two excerpts I found in my notes:

March 6, 2015

I believe that God has ordained this time in my life to show me His glory magnified in my life. I went from making $95K a year to a stipend of $359 a week. In this situation, most people would be stressing out. I am just standing on God. The funny thing is that I paid off three bills since I have been laid off oppose to when I was working I was spending money on things that wasn't important. I have about two and a half months left on unemployment before the money runs out. By the grace of God, I have enough money in my bank account to make it a couple of months. I want to testify on the mercy that God has shown me these last couple of months. God has been keeping me and my family. My son has clothes, shoes, food, and shelter.

April 13, 2015

As I embark on my first ever fast over the next few days, I can say that God has truly blessed me. I have been out of work since November 7, 2014. I am truly blessed, because I was able to pay my car off in full. I am able to maintain all my bills that I currently have on time. God has held me thus far and He continues to be my Rock.

I can recall one day while I was sitting at a red light, I thought to myself I should run through the red light. For a quick second, I thought I was a bad mother, person, and someone who was incapable of obtaining a job. At that moment, I heard God's voice speaking to me and I didn't run through that red light. Shortly after that, I began to write my life's testimony which you are reading today.

Elise B. Gordon

"Let us not become weary in doing good, for at the proper time we will reap a harvest if we do not give up."
Galatians 6:9

"For ye have not received the spirit of bondage again to fear; but ye have received the spirit of adoption, whereby we cry Abba, Father." Romans 8:15 KJV

As I look back over my life I see all the trials, tribulations, suffering, distress, trouble, unhappiness, sadness, heartache, grief, sorrow, pain and anguish. I know it was only by the grace of God that kept me from losing my mind. God really loves me!

I had a good childhood. I was raised by my mom and dad, so I cannot tell you what it's like not having a mother and father in the home. I do not know what a girl goes through without her father in her life. So I cannot blame my short comings or my mistakes on my dad not being there, because he was there. We had a nice house, nice cars and both of my parents worked. My dad was a DC Metropolitan Police, so his work hours kept him out of the house a lot. He was the strong disciplinary parent, but also a hard worker. My mom was the nice one. She waited until we were all in school before starting her career. I have an older brother and two older sisters who lived in the home. (No step or half siblings) We also had police dogs that worked with my dad, but they were also our pets.

Sounds like a perfect family, right? Then why did I still have to go through my trials and tribulations? Why did I do stupid things in my life? Well, it all started when I realized I had a best friend. She went with me everywhere I went. I thought her job was to talk to me and help me get through this thing called life. I did not fight it, I was comfortable with her and how she led me. She had total control of my life. At the time, I did not know I could make choices on my own. In other words, I thought it was normal to be controlled by her. She was with me everywhere. I welcomed her in my life. I looked for her every morning. Her name was FEAR. The meaning of her name was nothing like I thought. Her name means an unpleasant emotion caused by belief that someone or something is dangerous likely to cause pain or a threat. I looked at fear so wrong. I thought she was a friend that loved me and had my best interest at heart! She still comes back to visit at times, but now I tell her: *"There is no fear in love, but perfect love casts out fear. For fear has to do with punishment, and whoever fears has not been perfected in love." 1 John 4:18 ESV*

Fear of Being Smart

"Oh, fear the Lord, you his saints, for those who fear him have no lack!" Psalm 34:9

All throughout grade school, I received the grades that fear wanted me to have. I never put my best foot forward; I was always scared to try hard or my best. I remember in the first grade, I did not understand math so I would go to sleep once we came back in from recess. I was afraid that I would say the wrong answers. I would never raise my hand to read or volunteer to go to the black board. Fear whispered to me that the kids in my class would laugh at me. So, I kept my hand down. Even if I had a question, I was afraid to ask or I would tell my friend Jamie to ask the question for me. All the way through the 12th grade I believed what fear said to me, that I was not smart enough.

One of my sisters and I are 13 months apart in age and she was so smart. She always made the honor roll. So since I never applied myself, all the teachers that she had once I got in their class they would always say to me, "You're sure not your sister, Elerie!" In other words, they were calling me dumb. So, I grew up believing that you are either born with smart genes or dumb genes, and I had the dumb genes. I would read all night, but I would never remember the information. I attended the University of the District of Columbia, which was one of the hardest times of my life. Fear had me feeling like a little mouse trying to go through a maze. I received credits, but I never finished college. Fear had me so confused. I did not realize what she had me believing was a lie, until I accepted my calling to ministry.

I had to attend Minister's Training at my church. She came to me again telling me, "Everyone will see how dumb you really are, because you cannot hide behind your smile and quietness". So, one day I went to tell my Pastor (at the time) that I need to withdraw from my calling and the class, but I was so fearful that I left his office without telling him. By this time in my life, I knew the Lord and His Word. So, I began to pray and seek God. I asked God, what should I do? Immediately, God told me that I wasted so much time believing fear, but I can still attend minister's training, I just need to study differently. So, I started to use index cards, posted notes, and my smart phone to record our trainings. I learned to listen to the recordings over and over. I also wrote down the information over and over. I had to look at the information over and over to obtain it. I started getting the highest grades in the class. It got to the point where one of the smartest guys in the class asked me how do I study, because my grades were higher than his. Who would have thought? Not me.

From that point of my life, I also learned that being smart is a choice. You choose how your life goes, not fear. When it comes to new things in my life, fear does show up but she doesn't have control over my life anymore. She is not from God. God led me straight to *2 Timothy 1:7 "For God gave us a spirit not of fear but of power and love and self-control". ESV*

Fear of Not Knowing My Worth

Isaiah 41:13 "For I, the Lord your God, hold your right hand: it is I who say to you, 'Fear not, I am the one who helps you'."

When I was a teenager, I thought if you like someone it was alright to have sex with them, I later found out that's a lie. I guess I never had the "Why You Should Not Have SEX" conversation. It

41

went more like this "DON'T HAVE SEX!" How many know if you tell a teenager not to do something they will do it anyway? We must express to our children their worth. We must explain to them why it is so important to wait for marriage. I did not know my worth. Instead of me being fearful of what my parents would say, I was more fearful if the guy would quit me (that was the language back in my day for breaking up).

I wish I could paint this picture and tell you the first time I had sex I got pregnant with my oldest daughter, but it wasn't. The first time I became pregnant was when I was in the 10th grade. I was so afraid to tell my mom and dad, but I was more afraid of becoming a mother. We went to Washington Hospital Center and I had an abortion. When I got pregnant with my oldest daughter, it seemed like fear was right there. I had already graduated from school and had my first job. I worked at Kapitol Daycare Child Center in Capitol Heights, MD. My daughter's father and I planned to get married, but one evening my life had changed. That was not the plan anymore. So now I had to raise my daughter by myself. Her father and I shared every other weekend, until he decided to move to North Carolina. My family was very supportive.

I remember my first apartment on Nova Ave. in Capitol Heights. We would hear gun shots a night, so I had to teach my daughter whenever you hear that sound to hit the floor and not to look out of the window. One night it was after 10:00 and my daughter was in her bed. Suddenly, I heard a gunshot. I called out to Shanice. She said, "Mom, I'm already down!" I also remember times when my daughter and I would go to McDonald's to get her a Happy Meal and I would not get anything to eat. I made her think that I wasn't hungry, but the real reason was I didn't have enough money for the both of us to eat. Being a teenage mother teaches you many lessons, but it didn't teach me my worth. If anything, I felt less than because I was a teenage mother.

Still not knowing my worth I started looking for love again. My dad was a DC police, so I started looking for DC Police. Later, I found out all the guys I thought I was in love with all had the same agenda. They would tell me I was the only one, buy me a few things just to have sex with me. Once I became aware of this repeated cycle, I valued never to date another police officer.

Fear continued to show up in my life, but my daughter and I made it by the Grace of God. We both gave our lives to God and became members of the Holy Christian Missionary Baptist Church for All People. I loved that church. It was there where I learned about self-worth.

"Casting all your care upon him; for he careth for you."

1 Peter 5:7

Fear of Dying

Before I got saved and joined church, I got pregnant again. But this time it was going to be different. To my surprise it was different. I was 7 ½ months pregnant when I got married, but it was all wrong. Fear had me so confused. I got married the first week of November, by Thanksgiving everything went sour. I will never forget on December 13, 1995 I woke up and didn't feel any movement from the baby that I was carrying. I was so scared that I stayed in the bed all day. My family told me to go see my doctor that next morning. My mom went with me to the doctor's office. The doctor and nurses tried their best to listen for the baby's heartbeat. After they were unable to find the heartbeat, they gave me an address to an office in Clinton, MD.

Once we arrived, they took me straight in back into a dark room for a sonogram. After the sonogram I went to sit in the waiting area, a few minutes later my doctor walked into the office. He came up to me to break the news to me. I couldn't even talk, all

I could do was cry. We lost the baby, and by this time I was 36 weeks pregnant. Doctor Lee told me to go to Prince George's Hospital and he will be there soon.

December 14, 1995, was one of the hardest days of my life. I had to deliver my baby as if she was alive. They induce me so that I would begin to have labor pains. I thought all of this was a waste of time. I could not understand the point of going through all that pain and for all those hours. I just wanted the doctor to cut me open and take the baby that way. As the hours went by, the pain got so unbearable and my tears were unstoppable. The doctor told me to push, so I started to push and push with every labor pain. I still could not understand why I had to go through this hardship.

Once the baby came, the nurse took her to clean her up and wrapped her in a little pink and blue blanket with a matching hat. She brought her over to me to hold. I stopped crying and started to look at her little face and hands. I began to talk to her. I told her I don't know why this happened to us. I told her I will always love her. I told her she has to go back to Heaven where the Angels are from…immediately, we named her Angel. I called on God, even though I did not have a relationship with Him at the time. I knew of God and His Son Jesus, but fear always kept me from having a real relationship with Him. But I called on Him. I promised Him if He gets me through this I will join a church and will be faithful to God's Holy Word.

Soon after I made that promise to God, Pastor Stephen E. Young Sr. walked in my hospital room. I told God that I will join the church. Pastor Young was amazing! I was not a member of his church and only visited one time, but he came to the hospital during an ice storm to pray with us. We all held hands in a circle as he began to pray. After the prayer, everyone left. I started to feel numb as if the nurses gave me some medicine to make me relax, but it wasn't a good feeling or maybe I was going into shock. I had

44

to say goodbye to by dear sweet Angel Venae, I kissed her face and said goodbye. They rolled me out of Labor and Delivery and into a room. The feeling of losing my baby had over taken me. I turned over in the bed and tried to go to sleep. My husband at the time thought I was asleep, so he gets on the phone. I started to listen and noticed he was talking to a woman. He asked her how her day was and about some of the children at the school where they both worked. The more I listened, the more I realized he was seeing her on the side. I just laid there as if I was asleep.

A couple days later, I was discharged from the hospital. I was so heartbroken. My arms were so empty. On top of all the pain I was feeling, the nurse gave me a real big ziploc bag full of pills/medication. Fear told me to take my life. She said, "Kill yourself!" I told her I don't want to die. I have Shanice to live for. She needs me. I shall live and not die!!! As soon as I was off bed rest, I honored my promise to God. I went to the HCMB Church for All People. I got saved and became a member of the church; I was faithful. I kept my promise, so God restored what I lost.

Before I got a divorce, God blessed me with another baby girl a year and a half later. I named her Lonise (Loni) Rene. So now I'm back being a single mother of two daughters and living with my parents. One thing about me, I always worked until the time I lost my job and my financial load became overwhelming. So fear showed up again, and told me I cannot take care of my girls and my mom and dad will give them a better life than I could. I believed her, but I should have known she was lying because my girls and I were already living with my parents at the time. I was receiving unemployment, but it wasn't much money at all.

I would share my sad story and guys would give me money. One day I was on the phone with my good friend (at the time) Shelton, and shared my sad story with him. Immediately, he asked me if I tithe. I told him, "NO! I can't afford to tithe". He told me I can't afford not to tithe. Back then I thought tithing was just giving my money to the church. In opinion, the church was doing fine. Why would I give my money to a church that is doing well? Shelton broke tithing down to me. He read and explained Malachi 3:8-9 which states "Will a man rod God? Yet ye have robbed me. But ye say, Wherein have we robbed thee? In tithes and offerings. Ye are cursed with a curse: for ye have robbed me, even this whole nation." The part that grabbed my attention was "cursed with a curse". That thing scared the mess out of me! I didn't want to rob God and I didn't want to be cursed. I let Shelton know the amount of money I was receiving from unemployment and he explained to me how much money I was to give for my tithes. After I started giving and studying tithes, my whole life changed! Within three months, I got a new job, new car, new apartment and I became my Pastor's permanent nurse. You must trust and believe that God is your provider and believe that His Word is true.

"When I am afraid, I put my trust in you." Psalm 56:3

Fear of Success

"So do not fear, for I am with you; do not be dismayed, for I am your God. I will strengthen you and help you; I will uphold you with my righteous right hand." Isaiah 41:10 NIV

Shelton and I became best friends. We talked all the time as friends. I wasn't his type and he wasn't my type either. So, it was nothing more between us. We talked about everything. If I had a relationship problem, he would tell me how to address the problem. I helped him with projects he was working on for business and ministry. After many years had gone by and once we were both out of our past relationships, something special happened. We decided to be more than friends. At this time in our lives, he was Minister Gordon. I took off the Minister part and started calling him Gordon. I shared my dreams with him about starting a child care business, but I was afraid. He encouraged me to sign up for the classes and he would pay for them. In 2003, I started the process of "How to Start a Child Care Business". Fear was right there, but Gordon encouraged me to believe in myself and that my dream would come true.

I took my classes at night and on Saturday mornings, because I had a full-time job with DC Child and Family Services. I remember 2004 being a busy year for me. I'm going to give you all the short version: In April, Gordon and I got engaged. This was also the same year my oldest daughter was graduating from high school. In June, I was let go from my job of three years. Gordon and I got married on July 31st. By August, I launched my child care business. During this time, Shanice was headed to Coppin State University in Baltimore, MD which was only 45 minutes from home yet she still stayed on campus. We were so proud of her. She was the first grandchild to attend college. In September, my husband and I found out we were having a baby. While all this was happening, Loni was adjusting to all of the changes very well. Once Shanice went off to college, Loni became lonely. She made her way in our bed just about every night until the baby came. I was so fearful and worried about Shanice being away from home for the first time ever. I made sure she called me every night before she went to bed, no matter what time it was.

The following year our son, Shelton James was born. I was so happy to have a son, because I had three girls. I honestly thought I could only have girls. Both sides of the family were so crazy about baby Shelton. He was the baby of both families. I had the day care so he was able to stay with me, until it was time for him to go to school. Little Shelton was so excited to go off to kindergarten. Once the first day of school came, his whole mood changed. He cried and didn't want to go to school. I had to write him notes every day. When he felt sad at school, he would look in his desk to read his notes from me.

One night in 2008, Gordon told me that God called him to Pastor. Instantly, my heart dropped. I started to think if I was ready to be a First Lady. By this time, I had three first ladies: the first one just sat and looked pretty, the second one looked pretty but she worked hard in the background and the third one looked pretty, worked hard in the background and sung her heart out during praise & worship and for the main selection before the Pastor preached. They taught me that a First Lady can have many assignments besides looking pretty. In April 2011, God used my husband to birth Better is the End Ministries. We have been in ministry for six years now and we are still doing the work of the Lord.

Fear of Not Having My First Hero

One Friday evening while I was closing up my day care for the weekend, my phone rang. Many people say when you receive bad news the phone rings different, but my phone rung as normal. My mother was on the other end saying, "Lise (which is short for Elise), can you come to the house? Something is wrong with your dad." Then she went on to say, "I called 911 and they are here now." I immediately called up the stairs to Gordon. We told Loni and Shelton we have to run to the store and we will be back. My parents' house is only about six or seven minutes away. As we were coming up Brookes Road, I saw an ambulance coming down the hill. The lights were on, but there were no sirens. Immediately, I felt emptiness. We arrived at the house, my mom came to the door saying she did everything she could. Once my sister, Elerie got to the house, we all got in Gordon's truck and headed to Prince George's Hospital. As we were on the way, I began to pray as tears ran down my face.

As we turned off of Addison Road onto Eastern Ave, Deitrick Haddon's Song "Well Done" came on the radio. It was like a sweet peace came upon me, it was like God was letting me know my dad was with Him now. As Deitrick started to sing *"I just want to make it to Heaven, I just wanted to make it in. I just want to cross that river, I just want to be free from sin. I just want my name written, lambs book of life. And when this life is over."* But when I heard Deitrick say, "Well Done" I knew my daddy was gone. It was like a confirmation from God.

When we arrived at the hospital, they told us to wait in a family room. As we waited, my brother, Elgie and my sister, Eldean came in, and then more family arrived. Once everyone was there, a doctor entered the room. He introduced himself and explained to us in medical terms that my dad had died. Everyone started to cry, but because of the peace I received from Detrick Haddon's song I began to praise God like never before. I screamed as loud as I could, "He made it in! He made it in!" I thanked God that He made it in with tears coming down my face I celebrated that my dad made it to Heaven. I was hurt, but the joy of my dad making it into Heaven outweighed the pain. The doctor let the family go in the back to view and to spend our last moments with my dad. Gordon and I went home to break the news to Shanice, Loni, and little Shelton. They cried so hard. It was tough for me to believe my dad was gone. My family and I were strong through the whole progress.

A few weeks later, after all the calls, text messages, and all the visits were over, I went into a slight depression, but no one knew. I would sit at my dining room table in the same chair every day and go blank. Then, it got to the point where I became mad at my dad for leaving me here. I would say, "How could you leave me? You were with me my whole life, what am I suppose to do now?" I knew this was not healthy, so I began to pray and fast. One day I sat in that chair and asked my dad to forgive me. I realized that was being selfish and only thinking about myself. After that, I was at peace again. My mother has been amazing since my dad's transition. Her strength grows stronger as the years go by. She has been a notable example for her children, grandchildren, and great-grandchildren. She has taught me how to be a good mother and grandmother. My husband and I have two beautiful granddaughters and wonderful son in love.

As I continue to look back over my past, I realize fear had me in bondage. I have so much more that I have gone through, but I know I can't tell it all in this section of the book. I just had to share how I learned fear is not my friend and it's not yours either. If you or someone you know is struggling with fear, I want to encourage you that you can overcome it too.

First, it's important for you to know fear is not from God. Fear is a spirit of bondage. It will enable you from following your dreams and walking in your purpose. What if I had lived my whole life in fear? I would have died a long time ago. Fear told me to take every one of those pills that the hospital prescribed me. I had pills for everything in the bag that they gave me. It was the enemy's plan for me to end my life, and he made it easy for me. Instead of the doctor giving me prescriptions to fill, they gave me the prescriptions already filled.

I didn't mention all the car accidents I was in. When Loni was six years old, we were hit by a drunk driver so hard that we ended up on the opposite side of the street after the car spun around a few times. I also remember when I was so scared to leave a crazy relationship with this drug dealer. I heard a voice say "go home", but I was afraid to leave. Fear also kept me from ministry. I would be so fearful to hold or speak into a microphone. Now I don't want to put it down. Overcoming fear is God's plan for us. One evening for Bible Class I taught on fear, and for home work I had everyone look up scriptures on fear and to memorize at least one scripture. So, when fear shows up they would have something to stand on (the Word of God). So, now as I close this section of the book, I encourage you to find a scripture on fear or whatever it is you may be struggling with, so that you too can stand on God's Holy Word.

Rhonda Dickerson

"I can do all things through Christ who strengthens me."
Philippians 4:13

Childhood

I was born on March 1, 1984, weighing only 2 lbs. As a result of me being underweight at birth, I developed a lazy eye in my left eye. I was told that I had to wear a patch over my right eye to strengthen my left eye.

At the age of two, I started living with my grandma. I remember my grandma always saying, "I came to visit and you walked out behind me and never went back". I also remember my grandma taking me to a little daycare in the bottom of a church until I was able to go to elementary school and they also had a before and aftercare program. I always loved school. As a young child, I always wanted to be a doctor or teacher. I attended J.O. Wilson Elementary School located in Washington, DC until I graduated June 1996.

Okay, let's back track a little. I was raised by my grandma, but some readers may be wondering where my parents are. As a child I never knew my biological dad and my mom was around, but living her life. I don't have many memories of my mother, but I remember seeing her a few times and one last conversation with her. Who would've thought that this would be one of the last conversations with my mother?!

Losing a Part of Me

I had a little sister who passed away at the age of 2 years old. According to her death certificate, she died from AIDS and congestion heart failure. She contracted the virus from my mother. I believe this is how my mom really found out about her sickness.

On December 17, 1991, my mother passed away and I really don't have many memories of her. My mother died from AIDS. At the age of 7, this was a lot to take in and I am not even sure if I dealt with it the right way. My mother was a drug addict and contracted AIDS that way. I believe this is when my anger started. I felt like I was robbed of childhood memories and experiences.

I am the second oldest child of six. We were all separated. My brother and I lived with my grandma, my older sister was raised by our great grandma, and my younger sisters were in foster care until they were adopted.

As the years went on and time went by, I was dealing with a lot of depression and anger. I went on with my daily routine as if nothing was wrong, but I was hurting deeply. My grandmother took us to therapy, but it wasn't what I wanted at the time. I didn't feel like anyone understood what we were really going through. As I was getting older, more feelings and emotions were racing through me. I now wanted to meet my father. I had so many questions for him.

At the age of 13, I remember begging my aunt and sister to set up something so that I could meet him. My sister and aunt set up the appointment and I met my father at Johnny Rockets in Union Station. When I sat down with him all he did was cry. I was looking at him like, "Why are you crying?". After about 30 minutes to an hour of meeting my father, I got up and left. I told my sister and aunt that I never wanted to see him again.

Meeting my biological father for the first time was very disappointing to me. I was left with voids that were worse than before. I *still* have unanswered questions.

Transitioning

Leaving elementary school and beginning a new journey in middle school became scary. During these adolescent years, I became extremely angry. My anger towards people started to escalate. I didn't care what a person said to me, I had to have a word to come back with. This anger was very traumatic and affected my 7th and 8th grade school year.

I attended two different junior high schools. The first school I attended I really didn't want to attend. I got into trouble every day. I acted out until my grandma removed me from the school. I really enjoyed my new school. I met some awesome teachers and friends that I still communicate with today. Although my school environment changed, my attitude towards life and certain things didn't change.

God has a way of placing people in your life who will change your life for the better. During my 9th grade year in high school, God placed an amazing woman in my life. Ms. Brown was my science teacher, but she became so much more to me. She was a mother figure for me. She made sure that I didn't mess up in school and if I did, she was right there to discipline me. Although these things were new to me, because I was so used to doing things my way (well, what I thought was my way).

Ms. Brown took me under her wings as a daughter and she didn't take this responsibility lightly. She stayed on top of my grades, communicated with my teachers, and when I got out of line with my mouth and behavior, she disciplined me. Before I left school to go home, Ms. Brown always made sure I had all I needed, corrected me for the things that teachers came to her and told her throughout the day. I am not going to say I always agreed with her or that I didn't cause problems, because I definitely did, but she never gave up on me.

The next school year God blessed me with another woman who had an impact on my life. Miesha Perry (Thompson) became my Physical Education teacher, who also cared about my education and made sure I stayed on track. Not only was Ms. Perry concerned about my education, but she also cared about my spiritual life. She invited me to her church, where I later became a member. Also at the age of 15, God placed a father figure in my life. Shelton Gordon became my God-father, but I call him my dad.

Something's Wrong

When I was in the 10th grade, my vision in my left eye started changing. I told my grandmother and she took me to the doctor. I went to my regular eye doctor and she kept telling my grandmother that I was being lazy and not forcing my eye to see. I had to go to another doctor for a second opinion. My grandmother and I went to a doctor in Waldorf, MD and found out that a cataract had developed on my left eye. I really didn't process all that was being said to me at the time, but I knew that I had to have surgery.

In early 2000, the cataract was removed and I lost complete vision in my left eye. So, now I only have one eye to do all the work. This became such a frustrating whirl wind. As years went on, I started getting discouraged about my dreams in life. How was I going to become a doctor or teacher? I won't be able to get my driver's license.

During this time, a teacher at my school started taking me to her church. I really didn't know much about churches. I went to church when I was younger but that's it, I just went. I knew there was a God. I definitely had faith, but I needed a closer relationship with God. Going to church and learning about God was something that I enjoyed. Although I didn't join any activities I wanted to be involved, but I felt like a misfit because I didn't know the Bible like the people that I was surrounded by. How do you go to your extended family and tell them you don't know the Bible? Where do you begin to read? I wrestled with these challenges, but still wanted to learn and know more about God and the Bible.

On October 20, 2000, I lost someone very close to me. Ms. Brown died from complications in a car accident. This was one of the most devastating things to me. Honestly, this death was worse than losing my birth mother, because I had the opportunity to spend time and create memories with Ms. Brown, then she was snatched away from me. My grades started declining after this for a bit, but I was able to pull it back together. I graduated from high school as the Valedictorian. I received a scholarship and went to one of my colleges of choice.

The Journey

In June 2002, life was all so clear. I knew my goals and I had dreams for my life. After graduating from high school, I was headed to my dream college, Johnson C. Smith in NC. I adjusted to the college life as a freshman well. Most importantly, I was doing great in my classes. I was averaging a 3.75 GPA. To some people it probably seemed as if I was doing good and wasn't missing anything, but in reality, I wanted to be home. In my heart, I felt like that was the hardest thing to tell my family. I didn't want to disappoint anyone, because I was so far away from home (Washington DC). Like most college students, this was my first time being away from my family and I felt alone. I think I should have waited a year before going away to college. So many thoughts ran through my mind, and because I didn't want to disappoint my family and friends, I kept these feelings to myself.

I came home for Christmas break, but I still couldn't bear to tell anyone how I was really feeling about being away at college. I honestly didn't want to go back to NC after my break. So instead of mentioning it to anyone, I returned to school in January. I started my new classes and that's when anxiety and depression really settled in. I started missing classes, making up work, sleeping in, and ignoring phone calls. I was really getting depressed. It was two weeks into the spring semester when I finally decided to attend my Speech class. On my first day of class, my professor assigned me and another student an assignment where we had to learn each other's background history and present it to the class. Well, that was on January 15, 2003, I received the assignment and never returned to class.

The guy would constantly email me and call my dorm room phone to complete the assignment. I wasn't too excited about the assignment, but I decided to go to the guy's room to complete the assignment so he could stop bothering me. We completed the assignment and I started resuming classes again, but the guy kept inviting me over to his room.

Sure, why not. There's no harm in watching movies and talking, is what I thought. Just to let you know freshman weren't even allowed in the male dorms. So he had me breaking dorm rules. On February 11, 2003, (which was also his birthday) I gave my virginity away to a guy I barely even knew. This was my first time encountering this type of temptation and I gave into it. This was definitely not the way I expected to lose my virginity.

After the act was done, I started avoiding people's calls even more. I felt like people started calling me non-stop. I felt like my dad and this lady from my church, Minister Dunn had me on speed dial every two seconds. Weeks later, I started feeling sick and wanting to just sleep. My dad was still trying to reach me and when he finally does, he starts asking some random questions (not really random but it's like he knew something was wrong). I came home mid-semester, because I was so sick. I still hadn't told anyone about what I had done. I was home for a few weeks, then months went by.

After two months went by, I finally went to the doctor's to take a pregnancy test. That was my first and last time seeing that doctor.

Have you ever been scared out of your mind?!

"Now I have to call South Carolina to tell this boy that I'm expecting."

"My family will be so disappointed."

So many thoughts ran through my mind after I received the news that I was pregnant.

At the end of the spring semester, I moved out of the dorms and back home to DC. I moved in with my sister, in her two bedroom apartment along with her and her two kids. It was nice, but being pregnant I just felt that I needed to get things going with my life. I stayed with my sister until I gave birth to my baby girl.

"Welcome Alaijah De'Nae Dickerson"

Alaijah entered the world on November 21, 2003 at 10:43pm. My sister, godparents, cousin, and best friend were at the hospital when Alaijah made her entrance. Being pregnant was a different feeling. I felt sad and very emotional after I had Alaijah. Her father was not helping me and taking everything as a joke. This became very frustrating and depressing. All I wanted for my child was to have her father in her life.

After I had my baby, I moved in with my cousin who lived in Kenilworth (DC). "This will be nice, at least we have our space", I thought. While staying with my cousin, I pretty much did what I wanted to do, but you know living with someone else there always comes rules or you feel like you have to walk on eggshells. Well, that's how I felt, like I just had to stay in my space, make sure it was nice and neat, be quiet as much as possible that is just how I thought it should go.

Things were going well at my cousin's house, until one tragic day. While Alaijah and I were taking a nap the building caught on fire. This was the scariest feeling ever. Trying to reach people and no one is answering or not understanding what I am saying. Alaijah and I lost everything! We only had what we had on our backs at the moment. It was an experience that I didn't know how to handle and be able to care for my two month old baby. In this moment of life, I really felt like I was on my own with no family or friends. I felt lost, confused, and like NO one understood me.

My Godparents allowed me to stay with them. I stayed with them for about three months. It may have been longer...I really don't remember. I was content there, but I was still battling my own issues. I felt like I still had to be on eggshells. I had to get up, take Alaijah to daycare, go to school, come home, and stay in my area. That was an everyday routine. Sometimes Alaijah would cry and I would go down in the basement so she wouldn't disturb everyone's sleep. I would get up so early to take her to daycare and stand at the bus stop crying, because I felt like no one understood what I was dealing with. I am living with my Godparents, but I had so many thoughts and questions running through mind. One question was: "Why didn't my grandma take me and my daughter in? I have to get up so early, I really can't do this anymore, I want to end my life, and someone else can take care of my daughter. It is just too much to bear." I was dealing with so many thoughts and feelings with no escape.

Depression set in very heavy. "I have to leave!!!" I moved in with my grandmother, but I knew I couldn't stay there long either. I needed a plan, but until I came up with one I stayed with grandmother.

Growing Child...

Alaijah was a busy little infant and growing child. I received so many phone calls from school. I dealt with school suspensions, which made me very frustrated. I cried most nights, because I am sitting here trying to raise a child as a single mother and her father couldn't understand that he needed to be an active parent.

In the early ages of her life, my life had become a constant battle with her father. To be so far away, we argued so much. Despite our ill feelings towards one another, I still took my child to SC to visit him because she needed her father. She needed what I didn't have and that's all I could see and that's all I wanted for her. I traveled to SC every three to six months against family wishes, but all I could say was "My child needs to know her father". After Alaijah's 2nd birthday, I decided I wasn't going to keep traveling to SC, because he was not putting in any effort to travel to DC to visit his (only) child. It was difficult traveling with an infant by bus and train, but I was determined for her to have a relationship with her father. Over the years, I've learned that you can't force a person to be a parent.

I was residing with my grandmother, going to school, and working 12 hour shifts at a company called LaPetite Academy. I was starting to adjust to my schedule of working, attending school, going back to work, picking up Alaijah, and going home. This was my daily routine on public transportation. It was a lot but I had to do what I had to do as a single mother, because I wasn't receiving any financial help from her father.

The Move

I decided that I was ready to move on my own. I thought, "I have a child, I can't live with my grandmother forever". I moved into my first apartment in Forestville, MD. I was so happy that I finally had my own place for my daughter and me. I no longer had to walk on eggshells anymore. I thought life was sweet, but then things got out of control. I allowed my cousin to stay with me and she watched my daughter while I worked at LaPetite Academy. I cut off all communication with a lot of my family just trying to escape reality. I was trying to escape the depression that I felt and the anxiety from trying to figure things out. After being in the apartment for about eight months, I called my grandma and asked if my daughter and I could come back to live with her. Now my plan was to save, get a good job, and finish school.

I am back with my grandmother life is sweet, so I thought. I still felt uneasy. I needed my own place again, but I stayed with my grandmother for two more years.

People may have looked at me and said "She has it all together", but "together" was an understatement. In reality, I was dying on the inside. I was miserable and so depressed with life, but I kept pushing and pressing on because my child needed me. A whole year of me standing strong on my decision of not taking my daughter to SC had gone by, before my daughter's father decided he will come to DC to visit her. He came into town but it wasn't the visit I expected. My daughter's father and I "met up" and my second child was conceived. Please don't ask me why I slept with him, because still until this day I don't know the answer. One thing I can truly say is that my girls mean the world to me and I wouldn't trade them for anything.

Two days later before he left DC to head back to SC, I had already told him that I know I am pregnant. I decided that I wasn't going to tell anyone about this pregnancy, because I didn't want to hear anything negative from family and friends. I also decided it was best to keep this pregnancy a secret because my grandmother had already told me that I couldn't bring anymore kids into her home. So I went to work as usual, but I stopped going to school because it was too much trying to juggle school and work. Their father had assured me that this time around things would be different. He kept telling me, "I am coming for the birth" and "I will send financial support once a week". Everything sounded good, but I went on with my life as usual; the hard working mother.

Keep in mind I was still keeping this pregnancy a secret. I thank God that I wasn't showing. In September 2007, I finally decided to leave LaPetite Academy to pursue other dreams like going back to school, but my grandma was talking about retirement in a few months.

On January 14, 2008, my baby girl Aniyah Danielle arrived. The father did not show up as promised. Now, I have two kids, still living with my grandma, and facing new challenges in my life. Alaijah was in elementary school, but I felt like I was in elementary school. I received so many calls home from school, she got suspended, and she was just out of control. You're probably wondering "How does a 4 year old get suspended?"

I can recall the time I was disciplining Alaijah and noticed she was non-responsive for a few seconds, then came back to me and said "What did I do?". In March 2008, Alaijah was diagnosed with seizures. She was having about 90 seizures within two minutes.

Finding out this news about my oldest daughter was devastating. How can I help my baby and take care of a newborn? So much had transpired in this one year. In October 2008, Alaijah was diagnosed with ADHD (Attention Deficit Hyperactivity Disorder). The doctor prescribed her medications to help. I became overwhelmed with weekly appointments with a hyper 4 year old and an infant. Although these challenges aroused in my life while caring for my children, I still kept moving forward to reach my goals.

Another Set Back

Two years had gone by, and then I noticed that Aniyah still wasn't talking. I started researching, having hearing test done, and early interventions as well. With the guidance of the schools and doctors, I found proper care to help with my daughter's speech.

Aniyah started talking at 3½ years old. Then, I found out she was having seizures as well. This time around it wasn't as hard to deal with, because I already knew the procedures and protocol. I was truly dealing with a lot. For a long time, family members assumed that I was just medicating my children to avoid dealing with them, not knowing what I was really dealing with.

I constantly moved every year with my daughters. Every year it was a different reason, but they all seemed to tie together somehow. One year lights out, another year lights and gas off and another year the rent and utilities were just too much and I wasn't really working much. It was hard to keep a job, because I had to make sure my daughters were getting to their appointments and available for meetings with the schools.

Every time I felt like I was making progress, it was like I was being pushed back. I can recall saying "God, what am I doing wrong? God, I know you won't put more on me than I can handle."

"No temptation has overtaken you except what is common to mankind. And God is faithful; he will not let you be tempted beyond what you can bear. But when you are tempted, he will also provide a way out so that you can endure it." 1 Corinthians 10:13

I didn't give up, but I kept on pressing forward. I just needed to get a plan and execute it.

I am going back to school.

I am going to get my driver's license.

I am going to get back in church.

I will get a place.

I will have the finances to be able to maintain everything.

These were all my goals from 2014. As I started writing my plans down and working towards my goals, things started looking up. My housing came through in July 2014 after being on the waiting list for 10 years. I graduated from Med Tech Institute with my Medical Assistant certification on April 25, 2015.

God is so faithful even when we fall short.

Do you remember when I told you that I was feeling bad that I wouldn't be able to get my driver's license because of my eye?

"The Lord answered, If you had faith even as small as a mustard seed, you could say to this mulberry tree, May you be uprooted and be planted in the sea, and it would obey you!" Luke 17:6

I prayed that I would be able to get my driver's license, because this would help me maneuver a little better. I set a goal, but I did things a little different in the process because I wasn't quite ready. In December 2014, I purchased my first car. I was so excited, but never been behind the wheel. I took a driving lesson in December and never went back. In January 2015 while sitting at work, I decided that I will just step out on faith, pick a date, and take my road test. I was so nervous when I was about to take the test. On February 12, 2015, I took my road test and passed on the first try.

In March 2015, my oldest child was admitted to the hospital. This was a draining experience, but something that needed to happen in order to help my child. At the time, I was working at Sheppard Pratt Health System, which is a hospital based school for children with disabilities. Although, I worked with kids with disabilities on a daily basis, my job wasn't understanding that I needed to be available for my children too. I had to make an ultimate decision whether to keep my job or neglect my child's needs. I felt like every time I took one step forward, I was pushed a few steps back.

During this same time, I had a cousin who needed my assistance too. Although my cousin was not aware of what I was dealing with at work, I knew that helping her would be the perfect opportunity for me. I told myself that I was going to wait until the summer was over, and then I would resign or ask for part-time hours.

My last day at Sheppard Pratt Health System was on May 26, 2016. I decided that I would focus on some other goals and also be available for my children. On this same day, my cousin asked me to help her care for her child while she did training for a job. Amaya became a part of my family, I call her my bonus baby. She is such a happy and loveable child.

Out of all these obstacles I faced growing up, becoming an adult and learning how to be a mother to my daughters; I still kept the faith and never gave up. On October 26, 2015, I started my own business called From The Heart, LLC in the state of Maryland and a Non-Profit Organization called Soaring Above, Inc. in Washington DC where I assist families with transportation, I also assist families with children who have disabilities, and provide social and emotional support.

When I first started my transportation portion of my business, I started off with one client, and then my transportation clientele grew quickly. I hosted two Annual Back to School Drives in August 2016 and 2017. This was a big accomplishment to me and I was so glad they were both a huge success! I am looking forward to the 3rd Annual Back to School Drive in August 2018.

As I look back on my goals for 2014, I am happy to see that I have accomplished every single goal. I am also happy to say that I have been going to church faithfully. My youngest daughter, Aniyah is a member of the dance ministry. God has recently blessed my daughters and I with a house. God has been good to me and I am grateful that He used my testimony to encourage other women.

Shanice L. Stewart

"For I know the plans I have for you, says the Lord. They are plans for good and not for disaster, to give you a future and a hope." Jeremiah 29:11

Why would God use someone like me?

By man's standards, my past denies and disqualifies me from ever receiving the promises of God. By man's standards, I should never step foot in anyone's pulpit to preach the Gospel of Jesus Christ. I'm so glad I serve God and not man. I'm so glad God holds my life in His hands and not man. I'm so glad man does not dictate my destiny. I'm so glad I don't need man's approval or validation. Man would have given up on me a long time ago. Man would have labeled me as unworthy, undeserving and unusable, but I am so glad God is **nothing** like man!

Is that your testimony too?

For many years, I viewed myself just like man. The enemy had my eyes blind, my heart broken and my spirit bond. Sometimes we can be so wrapped and tied up in bondage and not even know it, but one thing's for sure, when you are walking in total freedom, you know it!

God removed the scales from my eyes, now I am able to see the beauty in my brokenness. I am able to see the purpose in my pain. I am now able to see the joy on my journey. God healed my broken heart, now I am able to completely love myself. Now that I am able to love myself, I can truly love others. God can take any broken heart and mend it back together like new. He is the real Heart Doctor.

Many times in life, we can find ourselves as our own worst enemy. When we allow the enemy to enter our minds, we give him control in the way we think and feel; the way we think and feel about ourselves, others and our lives. The enemy will have you comparing your life to other people's lives and not appreciating what God has blessed you with.

According to Philippians 2:5, "Let this mind be in you, which was also in Christ Jesus." It is imperative that we stay focused and keep our minds on the things of God. Don't allow anyone or anything to distract you from your destiny.

My Childhood

Growing up as a little girl without my father was very challenging. I knew who my father was because I spent time with him off and on as a young child. I remember more off days than on days with him. My father moved to North Carolina when I was about seven years old. As I grew older, I remember receiving three phone calls from my father each year. One call for my birthday, one on Christmas day, and the other call was to ask what I wanted for Christmas.

Every girl desires a relationship with her biological father. I believe every girl who grows up without her father imagines what it would have been like to be a daddy's girl. I know I always imagined what it would be like, because I never had the opportunity to experience such a great relationship. I cherished and looked forward to those few phone calls each year. I didn't hate my father, I just wished he was more active in my life growing up.

My mother raised me well, especially as a single mother. She sacrificed so much for me growing up. She did the best she could with what she had. In my eyes, she gave me the world. As a child, I had no idea we were struggling. In contrast, I thought we were living the good life. Not only did my mother make sure I had everything I needed, but she also gave me what I wanted. Honestly, I was a spoiled child. I had everything; nice name brand clothes, the latest and expensive tennis shoes and the best video games. I believe my mother made up for where my father lacked as a parent. In my eyes, she was the best mother in the world, not because of material things, but because she took great care of me all by herself. She loves me unconditionally, she supports my dreams and she pushes me to fulfill my purpose. She has set a phenomenal foundation of how to be a great mother and an amazing wife. That's why it is so important to watch what you say and do in front of your children, because good and bad seeds are being sown.

I am the woman, wife and mother I am today because of my mother. My mother always believed in me, but it took years before I believed in myself. The whole world can believe in you, but it won't do you much good if you don't believe in yourself. You will never fully go after everything that God has for you, if you constantly believe you don't deserve it. You can't truly live a purposeful life, if you don't know you have a purpose.

At the tender age of eight, I was touched and told to touch a female family member. Once this came to an end, I fell into the sin of masturbation and pornography. I struggled with this stronghold from elementary until college. Of course at the age of eight, I had no idea seeds were planted in my spirit until I got older.

Love vs. Lust

Growing up as a young girl without her father had its many challenges. I found myself searching for love in all the wrong places and people. I had my first boyfriend in 10th grade. At that time in my life, you couldn't tell me that he didn't love me and you couldn't tell me that I didn't love him. I had low self-esteem and believed everything he told me. At the age of 16, I wanted to "show" him how much I loved him, so I gave my virginity away.

Many years later, I came to the realization that it wasn't love at all but rather lust. Love doesn't hurt. Love is not conditional. After a few years, I found out that he was cheating on me and I was so mad. I broke up with him, but that wasn't enough for me. I wanted to hurt him like he hurt me, so I had sex with some random guy from my college. I was even more heartbroken when I found out that he had a nine month old baby during our relationship. This was one sign that I could not ignore. This guy hurt me so bad that I was done with all guys, because I thought they were all the same and I didn't want another guy to break my heart.

I was totally unaware the seeds that were planted at the age of eight started to grow. I found myself looking at females differently. Men couldn't fill my void, so maybe a female could. I acted out on my curiosity, only to find temporary pleasure. I was still broken and now confused about my sexuality because I enjoyed it, but I knew it was wrong. I prayed and cried out to God for total deliverance because I didn't want to have those feelings and thoughts anymore. I wanted to be delivered. I prayed for God to wash me with the Blood of Jesus! And He did.

At this time in my life, I did not know I was searching for someone who was right there all the time. I was running from the only One who could fill that void. God was the only one who could fill the emptiness that I had. God's love is truly unconditional.

The Power of Forgiveness

I lost my virginity at the age of 16 to my high school boyfriend. I got pregnant three times in high school and had three abortions. The first two were not my choice, but the last one was. I became accustomed to making my mess ups "disappear", but in reality it haunted me for many, many years. Abortion is such a touchy topic for many, because it's very hard for people to talk about even though it's very common.

For many years, I prayed and prayed for God to forgive me for what I did. I would become very uneasy when people mentioned abortions as if the word magically appeared on my forehead for everyone to see. I disliked myself because of my actions. So many times, I wished I could redo my high school years, because I would have saved myself for my husband.

As I was writing my manuscript for my first book, *Purposeless to Purposeful*, I was trying my absolute best to avoid this topic. I said, "God, I can't talk about that." He said, "You have to." I said, "I don't want anyone to know about that part of my past, I'm still hurt by it." God said, "Shanice, I forgave you when you asked for forgiveness. Now you have to forgive yourself." Once I forgave myself, the burden I carried for many years was instantly lifted from my heart, mind and spirit.

I finally felt free from the bondage that held me. Now I can minister to women and girls who went through the same thing. You are not your mistakes. God knew you were going to do everything you did before He created you, but guess what? He still created you. God created you on purpose, with purpose and He still has a plan for your life. Not only does He have a plan for your life, but the plans that He has for you are far greater than you could ever imagine! God is so amazing! He doesn't take our purpose away from us when we mess up; instead He gives us the grace to stay in the race. He's a Faithful God and we must be faithful to Him too.

Worst Decision Ever

During the summer of June 2008, my best friend and I decided to move into our first apartment together. We were so excited! Everyone else moved off campus their third and fourth year of college, so we knew it was time for us to move too! I was 22 years old and I thought I was ready to make grown-up decisions, but months later I realized I had made one of the biggest mistakes of my life. I thought moving in together would bring my best friend and I closer, but instead, it pulled us completely apart. If I knew this move would end our friendship, I would have gladly stayed on campus. Things didn't go the way we had planned and she was forced to sign herself off of the lease due to rent issues. I was left with a two bedroom apartment that I could barely afford on my own. My two jobs covered the rent, but I didn't have much money for anything else. Eviction notice after eviction notice was plastered on my door for all of my neighbors to see; although they didn't see me much because I was juggling two jobs and college classes.

I worked at CVS/pharmacy as a pharmacy technician on the weekends and at the Red Carpet Club at Ronald Reagan Washington National Airport during the week as a Hostess and Bartender. Things were becoming so stressful and depressing for me, but I didn't want to tell my parents. Everyone was so proud of me, I couldn't let them down. One day while I was working at CVS/pharmacy, this man came to the "drop off" window to ask a pharmacy-related question and then started to flirt with me. He gave me his number and I only took it to be polite, but I decided to text him a few days later because I was bored at my airport job. We talked to each other on the phone and through text for a few weeks. I shared my living situation with him and he told me that he knew someone who would love to be my roommate. With excitement in my voice I asked him, "Who?!" and he said, "Me!" and then I responded, "Oh no! I can't have some man living with me!" Because of my pride and desperation, I turned my back on my values and morals, and allowed this 32 year old married man to move in with me.

This guy and I became more than roommates pretty fast. Things were good. He was a great friend, we went out on dates all the time, he would help out around the apartment and most importantly, I didn't have to struggle to pay rent anymore. During all of this time, I was going to church and he would come with me occasionally. He even converted from Islamic faith and gave his life to Christ. Despite the major fact that he was still legally married, I thought I could mold and shape him into the man I wanted him to be for me, but I was sadly mistaken.

At this time in my life I didn't know God cared and loved me so much that He created a man just for me. When God creates something or someone just for you, you don't have to recreate them because God made them with you in mind. He knows who and what we need in our lives. People who make you better not bitter. People who help you not hurt you. People who push you closer to God, not pull you away from Him.

As time went on, things started to take a drastic turn. The issues that were once hidden began to come to surface. Once I realized that he was the jealous type, things started to become physical between us during arguments. One incident got so bad that I left the apartment in the middle of the night. All I had on was a t-shirt and some sweatpants, as I sat on my neighbor's patio in the dark. I felt safer out there, than I did in my own apartment. I said, "God, how did I get here?" Sometimes life moves so fast, especially when we make bad decisions after another. No one knew this man was living with me and I no longer wanted to live this secret life anymore, I wanted to be free.

In July 2009, while I was sitting at my airport job God spoke to me so loud and clear, "Milton is your husband." Huh? Milton is my what? I quickly thought to myself. He then showed me a vision of Milton's face. I had only seen Milton three times in my life. We walked down the aisle together in 2006 when my cousin married his brother. Milton and I were just texting friends. We alternated weeks where we would text each other daily scriptures and made a little small talk afterwards. When it was Milton's week, he never forgot to send his scriptures. When it was my week, sometimes I forgot to send him a text. When I realized it, I felt so bad because Milton never forgot about me.

I wasn't praying and fasting for a husband. I wasn't searching for a husband. I wasn't even thinking about a husband but once God said that, my whole life changed. I believe God had to tell me this news loud and clear because He knew my life was headed for destruction. I just sat there at work in total shock, because the more I thought about it the more I realized Milton is everything I ever wanted in a man. He's tall, dark, and handsome, loves and has a relationship with God and he's respectful. I was like "God, You are right!"

I didn't want to waste anymore of my life with someone who wasn't my husband. I knew I had to completely end this chapter of my life before I could start a new chapter with Milton. The guy definitely didn't take the news well. He did everything possible to try and destroy me and Milton's relationship before it even got started, but I'm a witness and know "What God has for you is for you!" and "No one can stop the plans that God has for you!"

The guy wouldn't leave the apartment, so I broke my lease and left. I was so happy to move back into my parents' house. It was definitely one of the best decisions I ever made. I may not have had a bed, but I sure had peace. Peace in my home and peace of mind. I was no longer depressed and stressed, I had joy again. I was excited about life again. I am forever grateful to God for pulling me out of my pit. I prayed for God to break and deliver me from every soul tie and to heal my broken heart from past relationships, because it would be unfair to Milton to fix a heart he didn't break. It's so important for us to seek God for healing before we bounce from relationship to relationship. God wants us to be whole and not broken.

Season of Brokenness

Now that I moved back home, I wanted to get my whole life completely on track. I knew the only way to do that was to totally surrender my life to God. I was still working as a bartender at the airport and deep down inside, I knew this was not the job God wanted for me. During this time we experienced many blizzards and snow storms, so the airport was closed which gave me an opportunity to stay home and enjoy some time from work. I found myself watching You Tube videos of different men and women of God preaching, praying, prophesying and worshipping God. I also watched videos of deliverance and healing services and crusades. I was so drawn to these videos, that I would watch them for hours and hours at a time. God used these videos to ignite a fire inside of me; a fire that I didn't even know existed.

It was in this season where God revealed my purpose to me. It was in my season of brokenness where God made me whole. It was in my season of brokenness where I fell in love with God. It was in my season of brokenness where I answered the calling of God on my life. It was in this season where I learned how to pray. It was in my season of brokenness where I totally surrendered my will to God's perfect will. I am grateful to God for my season of brokenness, because it built my character and integrity. Sometimes in life, God will break you down in order to build you up. It was in this season of my life when I learned that it is necessary to be broken before God. According to Psalm 51:17 "The sacrifices of God are a broken spirit; a broken and contrite heart, O God, you will not despise." (ESV)

I started spending so much time with God, especially my nights. I call them my praise and worship nights with God. During this time, I fell deeply in love with God. Not only did I tell God how much I loved Him, but I also showed Him that He was my number One. God desires for us to spend time with Him.

During one of my praise and worship nights with God, He instructed me to quit my job. I wasn't surprised at all; in fact, after those nights with Him I wanted to leave my job. I now desired to live a life that was pleasing to Him and not my flesh. I was honestly nervous about informing my supervisor about my "sudden" resignation, so I prayed for everything to work out smoothly. Once it was time to return to work, I immediately informed my supervisor about my resignation and he was very understanding. As I walked to the club, I was like "Wow God, you are amazing!" My last day quickly came to an end, so I increased the number of job applications I submitted. I couldn't understand why I wasn't receiving a call or email from any of the jobs I had applied to.

I thought because I was obedient to God by quitting my job like He instructed me to that I would find a job quick. After days, weeks, and months went by, depression found its home in my spirit. During all of this time, I was still spending my nights with God. Nothing changed besides the fact that I had even more time to spend with God, because I didn't have to go to work the next day.

In May 2010, I met a young lady at Milton's church and she was determined for me to travel with the church on their annual women's retreat. I wanted to go because I had never been on a women's retreat before, but I knew I did not have the money to go. She said, "God said you have to be there!" I thought to myself, "If God really wants to be there, then He will make a way." She called me later that night and told me that a few ladies at the church would like to sponsor me so that I could attend the women's retreat. God really blew my mind that day. I was so excited about attending my first women's retreat. Before I left for the retreat, I prayed that it would a life changing experience for me and that every woman would have a powerful and unforgettable time.

Forgiveness Equals Freedom

While on the retreat, I wrote in my journal and spent a lot of time with God when we weren't in our sessions and services. At one of our sessions, we were instructed to write a letter of forgiveness to any and everyone who had hurt us. I decided to write my letter to my biological father. As we wrote the letter, we had to envision the person standing right in front of us. Through words and tears, I released everything I had been holding onto since I was a little girl; the hurt, the pain, the challenges I faced because of his absence and how I truly felt about him.

Once we finished writing our letters, we were instructed to tear up the letter. Tearing up the letter symbolized that we truly forgave them and were finally letting go of all of the hurt we held onto. I honestly felt a peace of release as I tore my letter up. My heart was no longer heavy. I felt happy, I felt free. If you are holding onto unforgiveness from someone, I challenge you to complete the Forgiveness Exercise. Remember, forgiveness is for you! Forgiveness is the key to your freedom! Freedom in your heart, mind and spirit. Holding onto unforgiveness blocks your blessings from God. Don't allow unforgiveness to delay your destiny. God forgives us for our sins when we ask and repent, so why can't *we* forgive people?

Unexpected Blessing

During one of the sessions at the women's retreat, the Apostle was preaching and asked for me to stand up. I was like, "Oh no God, what is about to happen?" I am one who doesn't like attention and to be put on the spot. She proceeded to tell the women because I let go of my pride (at the altar call at the previous service), God was going to bless me. I lifted up my hands to show that I received the Word of the Lord. All of a sudden a lady yelled out, "Apostle! God told me to give her a job!" I was totally blown away! I was like, God, are You serious? Is this really happening right now? All I could do was cry tears of joy! I walked to the young lady who was so determined for me to attend the retreat, she was crying too! We hugged so tight and I told her, "Thank you so much!" Then, I walked over and hugged the other two ladies who made it possible for me to attend the women's retreat. My heart was filled with gratitude. The lady continued talking, "I've been interviewing many people for this position, but God kept telling me not to hire them". What God has for you, is for *you*! Here I was at home crying day after day, not understanding why God wouldn't give me a job, only to find out that He was working behind the scenes the whole time.

Sometimes in our lives it can look like God is not moving, but I want to encourage you and let you know that God is always working on your behalf. I know sometimes it doesn't feel like and sometimes it doesn't look like it, but God is always working behind the scenes and once He's done, He will present the blessing to you.

At this new job, I had my own office and my salary increased greatly compared to my past jobs. I was able to pay my outstanding college bill, which had prohibited me from re-enrollment the past year. After working at the Dialysis Center for a year, I was led to go on a spiritual fast for direction for my life. On the last day of the fast, God instructed me to go back to school. I had no idea that this would be the direction God would point me in, but I was ready to conquer my giant. The longer my break from college was, the more I grew comfortable with not going back, even though graduating from college was on my list of goals. My new supervisor encouraged me to go back to school, to the point where He scheduled my work hours around my class schedule. God showed me so much favor on this job, and He used me to be a light for Christ at this job.

In May 2012, I graduated from Coppin State University with a Bachelor's of Arts Degree in English. It took me way longer than I expected to graduate, but I am so grateful to God that He made a way for me. I was so blessed to have my husband and parents right by my side, as I walked across the stage four months pregnant with my oldest daughter, Melody. This was truly one of the best days of my life.

I want to take the time out to encourage someone who has been undecided about going back to school. You can do it! Just trust God and jump! Take the first step, and God will do the rest.

Husband from God

Not only does God know who we want in our lives, but He also knows who we need in our lives. When I was 14 years old, my church had weekly rap sessions for the young girls. My youth leader encouraged us to pray for our husbands, so I followed her directions. Even though I found myself in two relationships, I still prayed for my husband because deep down inside I knew these guys couldn't be my husband from God. Why? Because God will bless you with someone who lifts you up and not tear you down. Someone who makes you smile more than they make you cry.

I just want to encourage the single ladies who may be reading this to wait on God and don't settle for anyone less than God's best. It's ok to be by yourself. God wants to spend time with you before He sends your husband to find you.

My husband and I courted for two years until we became united as one. During these two years of courting, we abstained from sexual intimacy until we got married. My husband was actually a virgin when we got married and many times I felt like I didn't deserve him because I wasn't a virgin too, but God reassured me that He created Milton just for me. We serve a faithful God!

81

God has blessed me with an amazing husband and two incredible daughters who mean the world to me.

God Restores Relationships

Months after I wrote that letter and forgave my biological father for not being in my life, God began to restore our relationship. I was so excited to call him September 28, 2011 to tell him that I was getting married! He was so happy for me. Without me saying anything, I was glad that my biological father understood that my father would walk me down the aisle, because he couldn't give me away to someone he didn't even know. My husband asked for my hand in marriage from my father who has been in my life since the age of 13. My father is a Pastor, so he walked me down the aisle and also married my husband and I. It was such a major blessing and meant the world to me to have both of my fathers at my wedding.

My biological father and I went from talking three times a year to talking every other week! Only God! I really enjoy talking to him. God restored our relationship to where it feels like we never missed a beat. If it's God's will, He can definitely restore your relationship with your father, mother, siblings, or whomever. He is a Restorer.

Purpose

God doesn't take back His promises because you messed up. God doesn't change His mind about your purpose because you fell short. According to Romans 3:23, "…for all have sinned and fall short of the glory of God." Sis, we all have messed up, so don't let people make you feel bad as if they are perfect. We are all trying to live a life that pleases God and not our flesh.

Jeremiah 1:5 states, "Before I formed thee, I knew thee…" In other words, God already knew you were going to mess up and fall short. Before He created you, he knew you weren't going to do everything right, but He still created you! He loves you, with your flaws and all. God has given us the grace to stay in the race.

God knows every single thing about you because He created you in His image. God knew you were going to be a teenage mom. God knew you were going to have the abortion(s). God knew you were going to be promiscuous. God knew you were going to lose your virginity at a young age. God knew you were going to fall into the sin of lust, pornography, masturbation, and/or homosexuality; but in spite of it all, God still chose you! I pray for conviction and deliverance to take place even now as you read this. God can and will deliver you from any and everything that you are wrestling with. I pray for strongholds to be broken right now, in the Name of Jesus! I pray for a release of peace to overtake those who are broken and depressed. Your painful days are over! You shall receive the joy of the Lord!

God never ever wants us to give up. He allowed those things to happen because He knew you would overcome it. He knew He would/will get the glory out of your life! He knew your situation would help deliver someone else! Oftentimes, the things that we go through are not about us, but all those who are assigned to our lives.

God wants us to overcome EVERY obstacle in our life.

You are an Overcomer! You are Victorious! You win in Him!

Taneya Pair

"Trust in the Lord with all thine heart; and lean not unto thine own understanding. In all thy ways acknowledge him, and he shall direct thy paths." Proverbs 3:5-6

God Bless you and my prayer is that each testimony blesses you and encourages you. You are an overcomer

From Destruction to Construction, to God's Masterpiece

What happened to the lost girl who only wanted to be loved? What happened to the girl who has been hurt all of her life, who only wants to love someone regardless of the hurt that it causes her? What happened to the girl who only wanted love and attention from the ones closest to her, but never received it and ran to men and friends to find it? What happened to the girl who wanted the love that she had discovered over 20 years later, but as a child that person never knew how to love her? What happened to the girl who just wanted to hear "I love you", "I'm proud of you" or "I support you"? What happened to the girl who is unknowingly being battered and beaten from generational curses?

What happened to the girl who wanted her dad to love her and come into her life? What happened to the child at the age of 11 slept with cords around her neck hoping that she would die in her sleep? What happened to the girl who ran to sex and toxic relationships just to fill a void? What happened to the girl who put her plans and desires to the side to give the love and attention to her siblings that she never received? What happened to the young woman at her edge of depression, crying that God ends her life, rapid instant thoughts of running her car off the road and overdosing on medical pills? What happened to the woman who beat depression, completed two degrees, forgave those of her past and present? Not only did she find herself, but God turned her mess into a message and test into a testimony. I am she and here's my story.

As a child raised in a single parent home, you are exposed to the many faces of life (good, bad, and the ugly). Growing up my mom did her best of what she could with being my only parent. I never once despised my mom and I always loved my mom, but some things I didn't understand. I felt alone as I pulled my brother along and supported him. Later on in my adulthood, I understood things more and developed a greater love and understanding of our lives and relationship together. Many memories cloud my mind as I ponder on the days of watching children play with their parents, especially their dads. Daddy daughter dances, TV shows, and the worst of all Father's Day. Father's Day was a day that I would cry all day long from probably the age of 4 to 26. I would always think to myself, why doesn't my dad love me, why did he leave? Little did I know, the absence of my father not only made me feel that I wasn't worthy enough to be loved by a man, but even by God Himself.

At the age of six, I would search the yellow pages in hopes of finding my father or grandmother. I did this for years. I never hated my dad, but I always thought why did he neglect me? The thoughts began to fester into low self-esteem.

In the midst of it all, God sent me an angel, Grandma Jackson, who kept me every Sunday from the ages of 6-12. Grandma took both my brother and I to church with her. At the time I didn't have a full understanding of what was going on, but I just knew that I loved going and to be around her. This woman prayed over me and encouraged me throughout my childhood and adulthood.

Growing Pains

As a middle school child, I was broken. I cried wondering why no one would love me. I was verbally abused over and over for years and told that I would never amount to anything, but a "slut" and high school dropout. How does a 12 year old deal with that? These words came from the ones who I only trusted and respected.

As a teenager, I was lost. Losing my virginity at a young age, I had no direction, but only wanting to give love. It may seem awkward that I no longer wanted love. Being rejected as a child had a snowball effect throughout my life. I was so afraid of rejection of love that I just wanted to give it. Giving my body was my way of what I thought giving love meant. In middle school, I had a "boyfriend" who was older than me. Even though we weren't intimate, he would have me prance around in my panties and I thought doing that would make him like me. In high school, I thought sex was all I had to offer a guy. Throughout my youth years and early 20's, I sought validation from men. I didn't feel beautiful and was never told that I was. I never knew what love was, but I looked for it in all the wrong places, regardless of what it would cost me.

Relationships upon relationships upon relationships, there was a void that I was constantly running after to fill, from the verbal and physical abuse, to having an abortion.

The day I discovered I was pregnant, I was numb. As I replay the evening and how it happened, I began to think in that moment of what occurred to me didn't matter if this is what he wants I am going to lay there and allow it. I refused to provide names and proceeded to have the abortion even though I didn't want to. I had nightmares of hearing a crying baby and running to the crib to discover nothing there, to holding a blanket in the shape of a baby, rocking it to look in my arms and see nothing there. I had several breakdowns believing that I would never have children, because of I what I did. At one time in my life, I had to forgive not only the person who I was seeing at the time, but also myself.

Turning Tables

In my mid 20's, I finally completed my Bachelor of Science, and was on my way to grad school. Little did I know, I was walking into a life that would never be the same. After my baptism in 2011, within a week or so I returned to my life as I

87

knew it, sex, emptiness, hurt, and partying as I wanted and however way I wanted.

In January 2014, I came back to the same church I was baptized at and was ushered to the second row on the left center section. I was seated next to this amazing woman, Deacon Doris Felton and when Pastor opened the altar, this day was different. I began to weep after Pastor instructed us to squeeze the hand of the person next to us if we have a church home, but we have backslidden and want a fresh life with Christ. This woman embraced me and walked with me to the altar and that walk was the beginning of my new life.

From Brokenness to Newness

The day I came to Christ I kept hearing many people say all God wants is your "Yes", it began to be a thought like why do people keep saying that. A "Yes" what's so powerful about a simple "Yes". Little did I know or understand that the power in my "Yes" in obedience to the Lord was going to transform my entire life.

So my question then was, why would this powerful Being want a "Yes" from me? I have nothing to offer. I barley know who He is, but something inside of me knew who He was and I knew that I no longer wanted to live a life that I was living. I was angry, depressed, alone, ostracized, had low self-esteem, suicidal, empty, dark, lost, and in my eyes pathetic. I thought who am I that this Person wants to know me, let alone love me.

I was in a place where I was even afraid to accept that God wanted to love me. Me? Me? Is the question I would always ask myself.

But who was this young lady? What happened to her? How did she move from one lifestyle to the next, in what appeared to be within a blink of an eye?

In my transition, I joined discipleship and the devil began to attack my mind and all that surrounded me. My mom and I argued more than ever before, I attempted to stab myself in the stomach until my mom grabbed hold of me and stopped me. In that day she apologized and relegated on how not being there for me damaged me. I left home and slept in my car and no one knew. Not even my co workers. While I stayed in my car, I prayed for God to help me love my mom and forgive her as He wanted me to. I prayed and cried in my car for days that He would change our hearts. I also prayed that wherever my dad was, that He would change his heart and reconnects us when He's ready. The same year I decided to seek help after countless days of being depressed and losing 30lbs in a month and a half time span. I discovered that I was suffering from major depression and for a long time. I masked my depression, because I always wanted to be the one to give love even though I had no idea what it really was. Depressive thoughts were normal to me, and anything outside of it was beyond what I believed that I could experience.

I returned home, cried out to God, and this time it was no longer "Lord, let me die! Let me leave this life, because I don't want it anymore!" On a rainy evening in December 2014, I fell to my knees and cried out to God with my hands lifted. I said, "I surrender, I can't do this on my own, I can't hide my pain and I won't". The next following days, I noticed there was a shift that took place in my life, but the greatest test was that following February. In February, I was terminated from my job. In April, I totaled my car in an accident. In May, I failed the most important exam that determined my graduation and completion of grad school.

In the midst of the madness, I looked at every situation as a shift from me in my growth with God. Not once did I fall into depression. Yes people asked if I was ok or what was I going to do, but I had greater confidence in the Lord than my situations. I continued with discipleship classes, and those powerful praying women were divinely placed in my life to keep me on track. They prayed me through my first year and they are still praying me through. We prayed each other through.

In August 2015, I completed my Master's Degree in Clinical Mental Health. God saw fit that I would graduate. I applied to jobs left and right, and went to stay with my best friend, Georgette in NC. I stayed with her for one month, and in that time God gave me a vision to begin beading. As of today, this vision is slowly becoming a business. I've never had training or used inspirations from other designers. The Holy Spirit led me and I went forth. As of today, I have over 95 pieces.

I'm reminded of two scriptures, Philippians 4:13 "I can do all thing through Christ Who strengthens me" and Proverbs 3:5-6 "Trust in the Lord with all your heart and he shall direct your paths". These two scriptures saved me when I was dying in deep depression. Well as I went through the verses that I highlighted in my Bible app, I stumbled across Isaiah 43 which states: "When you go through deep waters, I will be with you. When you go through rivers of difficulty, you will not drown. When you walk through the fire of oppression, you will not be burned up; the flames will not consume you" (Isaiah 43:2).

This is exactly what God promised to do for Jacob. God did it for him and He has done it for me. Every difficulty that I went through, God sustained me and gave me the strength that I needed through Jesus Christ and with the comforter, the Holy Spirit. I made it through.

Purge the Old to Walk into the New

On January 10, 2016, I remember praying and telling God that I wanted to go to a greater level in Him. I kept a bag of exotic toys from a person I was dating in my past thinking that he and I would someday use it again even though we were over. God instructed me to remove the things in the duffle bag. Then, He said to get rid of the entire bag. I obeyed Him and that following Saturday I attended a Prayer and Prophetic Conference with my dear friend, Shanice. While at the conference, I received the gift of speaking in tongues. In that same month, I received my Master's Degree during the commencement and applied for the trade name of my jewelry business "Cherish" and landed a job within my field of Mental Health.

After the prayers of my Pastor, First Lady, amazing mentor Ray Nelson, best friend, mom, Grandma Pair, Grandma Jackson, and the presence of my dad in whom I connected with on Father's Day of 2015, life began to shift. I overcame the past and current season of hurt, pain, and agony. My life is forever changing and growing, until the day God calls me home.

Single and Simply Living

One of the main struggles I dealt with between the ages of 5-26 was wanting to be loved. I battled with understanding who I was, my purpose and also the meaning and action of love. Throughout my adult years, I watched friends and family move forward in building families to the point where I became depressed. Not once did I envy any of them, but I thought why not me. Am I not worthy enough to have a serious relationship? Can I not be loved? It was to a point where I thought well if my father couldn't love me, what makes me think anyone else would? Because of this I cried and found myself depressed for years thinking I wasn't enough. The problem was I didn't know who I was. The moment I surrendered that day in December 2014 was the starting point of me seeing how worthy and beautiful I was in the eyes of God. I began to see how I still had soul ties, and that was a purging process that lasted until January 2016.

God began to show me my worth, purpose, and true beauty. He continues to show me as I humbly accept it. He also showed me the areas of my life that I needed to make changes in. The day I said, "Lord, allow Your will and not mine to be done in my life", interest and desires began to change. I was no longer living to find Him, meanwhile wondering why I can't receive consistent true love, my desires became His desires. I no longer felt the need to sleep with a former partner to feel needed or wanted. I no longer felt that dying, urgent need to hear the words "I love you" or "You're beautiful" from a man. I finally discovered the Love of God. His love allowed me to love others and love them the right way. I had to purge from old things to receive new. Was I tested between the times? Absolutely! I was tested by severing "friendships" that were clearly outside of the will of God. Surrendering my desires to receive God's desires and expectations of me wasn't easy. Honestly, it was a challenge but I know what God has and wants for me is beyond greater than what I could've received in a thousand years. So I laid there after reading a chapter in the book "God's Best", the Holy Spirit led me to pray to God that He intercedes for me to break these soul ties.

I didn't know how severe emotional soul ties could be, especially if you've been emotionally involved with someone. I prayed for everyone from my past and present, even if the tie wasn't clear to me that it existed, I still called it out to God. Before I knew it, I still had ties to a total of five men. I began to pray in tongues and began to envision each man was before me with like a wide cord attached to me. I stood before each man and spoke in tongues and cut the wide (red) cord. However, prior to doing that, I could see each and every tie that was connected to me, to the ties of sexual fluid exchanges to being emotionally drained by placing them before myself. Giving them the benefit of the doubt, while keeping them around, answering and replying to every text message, I was continuously being passive aggressive. I could see all of these various ties and strongholds from them being picked and pulled from me. I then cut the cord and slammed five doors that were in front of each man.

After doing that, I felt pressure from my stomach while speaking in tongues and I began to lose my breath. I felt exhausted. During my first full year of discipleship, several times I found myself repeating the same cycles of fornication as I had in my past. I discovered my desire to break away from these cycles, though it was extremely challenging. I prayed and God revealed to me my truth and the ties that I had attached to my life.

Following the prayer, I remained bold and confident in God and continued to seek His will and directions on dating. I was no longer answering the late night calls and text messages or sleeping with a man to feel loved. God showed and gave me a love that filled that missing void and place in my heart since childhood. God showed me my beauty, strength, and boldness.

As I reached a point of confidence in the Lord, of course the devil started lurking around. The first guy that really hit my "wow moment" was one who I met while working in the community in 2016. I immediately began to think, Lord is this really You. I was reminded of how my husband and I would meet. Immediately, I noticed the exact physical description of what I asked for…. Pause…. No, I'm not shallow and yes I did kind of ask for specifics when it came to my husband, even to the physical appearance.

I on the other hand, was tired, hair twisted whichever way, eyeliner running to my cheekbone, and lips were probably chapped who knows. Nonetheless, he approached me, introduced himself, and we exchanged contact information. We conversed for a week. One day we sat and talked, and I told him I love the love he has for the Lord and I'm serious about Him and my spiritual connection with Him too. I pretty much put everything on the table. He said "You're young and different from some of the women that I've met but I like it". Long story short, I didn't hear anything else from him until months later, which I ignored because in that experience it was my first time laying before a man who was a portion of what I asked God for, but I was exposed to the question of what matters the most. Is his career, stability, charm, handsomeness and mostly the way he found you more important than his relationship with Me? Are My desires a priority to you? Will you compromise My desires for something that's only temporary and has no complete significance in your life? Will you forget Me? After I naturally laid down where I was and where I'm pushing to be, God asked me these things and I felt empowered and satisfied that I kept my truth with God beyond man.

When you see your Beauty as God sees it, all things will fall in line. You discover your worth. You discover your power. When I limit myself, I limit God. There were no longer limitations. I was no longer thinking I wasn't good enough to be married or have children. I moved forward in my life, understanding that I wasn't ready to be married at the timing that "I" wanted it to. God had more that I needed to do and release before my husband would find me. Between now and the day I turned everything over to God, my life transformed. My desires were "Lord, how do You want to use me. Take me and mold me as Your daughter." I fell in love with a love that is greater than anything anyone could give. I understood my season and continued to walk in the will of God. He gave me the peace and security I always needed and wanted, but never received. When the time comes God will release me to my husband. In the mean time, it's just God and I rocking and rolling.

Waiting and Growing

It is important to understand what love is before running after it. How can you run after something that you don't know

94

about or haven't truly experienced without the aid of a "significant other" or "special friend"?

If you haven't already, take time out for yourself.

There are a lot of people who are still clueless on love and I'm not just talking about the singles. In my opinion, your partner can not make you whole when you're broken entering a relationship. Take your time and allow God to do the mending of your heart and provide you peace of the spirit before taking things to the next step.

Who knows maybe there's a business, ministry, career change, change in location, or places to travel that has yet to be birthed from you.

Bring more to the table than an affection of a "potential healthy partnership", bring more to the table than brokenness or heartache, bring more to the table than your body. What can we bring to the table TOGETHER to get this thing started?

The greatest thing any person can do, whether single, in a relationship, engaged, or married is having an understanding of who they are and allow those very things to bring the two together to create something healthy and powerful with God front and centered. If God has unfinished business with you, don't rush.

Dating the Wrong Person

Dating outside of the will of God can place anyone at risk of nearly losing their God given gift. I remember browsing a post on Facebook that referenced the scripture, Proverbs 4:23 "Guard your heart above all else, for it determines the course of your life" (NLT). I was immediately stuck. I was immediately taken back to the days when I was sinking in sin, the nights that I cried to God, because I was hurting from hurting Him. I was instantly reminded of how precious and significant God's hand in my life really is. So many times we fail to understand or see how detrimental being with the wrong person can be to our calling. God's desire is more important than our desire or reasoning with someone's feelings. You can not be in something and remain there, that is not pleasing to God or conducive to what and where God is preparing to take you. At all times we must guard our hearts above all else, because IT DOES determine our course of life.

In battling guarding the heart, one must think "Is my life and destiny constructed by man or God? Is my purpose for man or God? Am I giving man who serves no significance or power to God, am I giving them the ultimate authority over my destiny and how and when it shall manifest?"

Relationships can either push you closer to God, to build a stronger relationship with Him or push you further away from Him. If your partner is not seeking after the will of God, pushing and practicing daily to live a life pleasing to Him, seeking and operating in their calling, respects, embraces, and encourages your calling, then you need to chuck the deuces and roll out.

When God is not in your relationship, there's no winning. In this race I'm bound to win through Christ. Being single is not a risk; it's a powerful choice that I know without a doubt will be pleasing on the end. A risk is taking a 50/50 chance and you're unsure. Not this. God continues to do exceedingly abundantly above all that I could ask or think and as His outpour of wisdom, love, direction, and blessings continues. I'm sure of that and I stand firm, excited, and sure in my choice during my time of being single, which will not be long. Keep your heart guarded, souls are waiting on your purpose to be fulfilled and manifested if it hasn't already. Being outside of the will of God will cause you to fall off track. The risk of drifting outside of God's will to satisfy flesh is not worth it.

I've had moments in life where people would challenge me by asking questions about the level of ability to fulfilling duties as a mother or wife, which I don't take offense to.

I was asked you weren't raised with the examples of how to be a wife or a nurturing mom, how will you be able to when the time comes? This was an unexpected question, but nevertheless, it was a great question. When I was asked this question, I wasn't offended regardless of whom it came from. I did tell the person that the Holy Spirit knows me well and I didn't get this far on my own, so I know whatever I lack God will provide. My relationship with God is the foundation and structure that guides and molds me. God has placed me in the presence of many powerful mothers, wives, and teachers. The reason why God has pushed me in such a short period of time is because as my mentor Ray says, it's "because you're teachable". My life is to please God in every area of my life, so my spirit remains open to His provision and molding.

During the first year and a half after rededicating my life to Christ, I asked myself the question: How will Christ accept me and love me when I didn't grow up as most people did knowing Him? How will He accept me when no one laid a firm foundation for me? Yes, my Grandma Jackson took my brother and me to church with her between the ages of 6-12, but I didn't know what it really meant or was able to grasps who Christ was. My pondering question was, how will Christ accept me when I didn't know how to study the Bible, let alone worship? How will He look at me? I wasn't worried about others, I was concerned about how will this Man of so much power that I barley know about welcome me. I'm not good enough to be in His presence. There were moments that I caught myself being frustrated with my mom, because I felt that she failed me of not leading me to Him or showing me how to live a life pleasing to Him. I had this zeal about Him without knowing who He really was.

I say these things to tell you, yes I came from a dysfunctional family that was unstable in many ways, but some families are. At times you take the good with the bad and keep it going. No, I wasn't raised in the church, but I rededicated my life to Christ as my Savior completely on January 28, 2014. I didn't come in with a foundation, but I knew there was something that I lacked and a missing piece of my life that only Christ could fill. It wasn't easy due to fighting depression, fornication, and self-doubt. I felt that I wasn't worth the time of Christ, because everything was unstable. I didn't have that direction as a child so to battle these things as an adult, I felt worthless.

But God knew what He was doing all along. On January 18, 2016, I received the gift of speaking in tongues, God has revealed visions to me, He has pushed me to complete grad school and placed me into my career four months after walking across the stage. God has given me the opportunity that I not only provide hope and encouragement to the clients that I work with, but also within my office. His light is luminous in my work place. God has also blessed me and used me to co-facilitate one of my churches' women's discipleship classes. God has also placed me in areas and filled me with the wisdom and knowledge of what it means to be a wife, supporter, nurturer, submission and most importantly, a woman who loves to pray and worship God.

None of who I am came from man. None of whom I've become was going to be derailed, because I didn't come from the common background of many.

There's room for you too in the heart of God and I don't care what you lacked during your development years. There is no age limit or bracket when it comes to running after Christ. There's no sin too great for Christ not to open His arms and heart to you. You are His selected and chosen, own it and embrace it. You're more than enough!

The Rose

When I think about concrete, I think about loads of pavement that lies upon soil for the purpose of driving or walking over with the support of pressure. As I reflect on my life, that's exactly how my life was. It was like concrete was laid over my life to keep me buckled under pressure and from discovering my purpose.

A rose grew from that concrete and in the troubles and challenges, not one moment was that powerful enough to snatch her from the root to discord her. God allowed me to grow and develop quickly before anyone could really stop to witness what was going on. Over the pressures that surrounded me, the confusion and busyness of life that occurred during that time, God kept me and allowed this beautiful rose to blossom.

You are a rose. You are unique. You have a special gleam about you. God made you and your situations uniquely for you. You are a child of the Most High God and He loves you more than you'll ever know. You are not a mistake. You are not a waste of time. You are not exempt of discovering real love, just because it wasn't shown to you. God saves and protects the fatherless, the hurt, and damaged. Nothing happened in your life that God didn't see coming.

For the fatherless, God selected your parents regardless of the situation or how you were conceived, because He knows that you were going to be the one to change lives. As all of God's children, He knew what your testimony was going to be when you were in your mother's womb. God knew your story and how He was going to use you to save people who are dying spiritually in this chaotic world. So if you don't feel like it now or don't understand how, in time you will as you continue living and following the Lord. You'll begin to say "Thank You" and be honored that it was me instead of "Why me?" God knew who you were before you were born, and He already had your purpose and story mapped out. God is not going to lose you, reject you, nor ignore you. He knows and He loves you. A rose that grew from the concrete; there's room for you too.

Forgiveness

Unforgiveness harbored in my heart against various people in my life. I never thought about how major being unable to forgive something or someone could have an impact on my life. I had no idea that I was doing more damage to myself, than I was to the person or the situation. Being unable to forgive any situation or person you have given it more power over you than you know.

Open Question:

Has someone done something to you and you resented the idea of forgiving and letting God deal with it completely? You can pray about a situation, but when you continue to interfere and not allow God full access and control, you'll remain in the same spot.

You can say "It is what it is" or the famous line "I'll just cut them off" and think you're done, but you're not. Forgiveness comes from a place of power and authority. Forgiveness shows that no matter what, I respect my God and His expectations of me than to allow this unforgiveness to linger. God moved me to a place where I had to forgive the person, because I couldn't allow the hurt which developed into bitterness to take residence in my heart.

Christ is the greatest example of showing forgiveness. His assignment, His reverence, His love, His commitment, and His purpose was more important than the sticky situations that we've asked for Him to enter. Christ looked at our sins and said no matter what you have done, I have laid My life down to save you. You've turned your back on Me, I have forgiven you, your unkind thoughts, forgiven, the moments that you went to everyone else but Me, forgiven. The times when I knocked on your door and you didn't answer, I forgave you.

Had we not been forgiven, where would we be? Had Christ not forgave those who hurt Him and He knew that they would, what progress or outcome would've occurred? What if Christ held onto the hurt and distanced Himself from us? What if He allowed the hurt to overpower Him and not fulfill His purpose?

Forgiveness is difficult at times, but it can have been worst holding onto what hasn't been forgiven. When you spend the time, energy, and attention to not forgiving someone, you will not have any energy to focus on moving forward.

As I think about spring, I think about spring in this sense of action and outcome. Spring in action means to jump forward or arise from. Saying to your past and/or present hurt, confusion, life changing situations; saying to those things "I have forgiven you" will allow you to spring forward into peace, power, and clarity. You begin to see the flowers bloom that were dead in the past season. You begin to hear the beautiful sounds of peace. You begin to see the light that was dimmed, because of times of unforgiveness.

Forgiveness will save your life and it already has. But the forgiveness that we must practice is forgiveness of others and situations that we clearly don't have control over. You can't control the power that it has over you if you haven't called it out in prayer and released it. The enemy comes to steal, kill, and destroy and his tricks are the same as they were thousands of years ago. But the power of God suppresses anything that is brought against you if you trust, believe, and take everything to Him in prayer.

When people hear my story or in your case read my story, after meeting me they become shocked. Some have mentioned that they assumed I've been in church all of my life or I've never faced the things that I have faced; but I did. God sent His Son as a sacrifice to give us a more abundant life. In the abundance of life, there's an abundance of joy and love. But with all great things there also comes great challenges. When I praise God, it's not always because I'm going through something, most times it's because I've made it through what could've killed me. I made it through stages of my life that could've consumed me and I would've never discovered my identity. My challenges allowed me to love others the right way, to know what love is, and how to receive it.

During my darkest challenges, I met the love of my very being, Christ. This loved allowed me to develop into a woman who could love her mom through her challenges and intercede for her. My mom and I have come a long way and that woman loves her some me and I love her too. I removed myself from the equation of what God was trying to do, I understood that it wasn't that my mom didn't love me, she just didn't know how to love me and it wasn't her fault. My mom has always been my rock and support. My mom could've let me go at anytime, but she didn't. She loves me as she knows how. God has done a change in her life in which I will forever be grateful for.

I am still a work in progress. From the completion of graduate school, to growing deeper in Christ, to watching my mom reach a place of peace, promoted within her career several times in one year with only having a GED or academic background, to me now co-facilitating a women's discipleship class and sharing my testimony without direction in my life only God could do it. My mom, dad, and I have grown to a place of love, forgiveness, and peace that only God could've created. My dad is like my favorite guy. I don't have a cookie cutter life. I didn't have anyone close to me pushing me through grad school in the days and nights I would stay in bed crying and depressed. I had people tell me that I wasn't good enough to graduate from high school, I wasn't good enough to have a nice job, and I wasn't qualified to be used by God. God uses the most ordinary people to do extraordinary feats, regardless of their backgrounds and short comings. The moment God grasps a hold of you, surrender your will in exchange for His will; that's it.

My life is a story created for God's glory and my life is no mystery. Only the one who endures to the end will win, and the power and spirit of the Lord is carried throughout their days. Nothing has occurred by accident. Everything was divinely orchestrated to share and I'm just some ordinary girl broken and pieced together for something greater than I imagined or thought that I was capable of carrying. God is love and if His love can transform my life in a span of three years and save me from over 20 years of depression, it is evident that nothing is impossible for God and He is limitless. I love you greatly and my prayer is that my story touched you as much as it touched me between the tears of joy and strength while sharing it with you.

About the Authors

Rhonda Dickerson is a native of Washington, DC. She is the mother of two wonderful daughters, Alaijah and Aniyah. She was also blessed with a bonus daughter, Amaya Savoy. Rhonda earned her Medical Assistant certification on April 25, 2015 from MedTech Institute. She is the CEO of From The Heart, LLC and Soaring Above, Inc. (non-profit). Rhonda rededicated her life back to Christ in 2011. Rhonda has a heart for giving and would do anything to make sure that the next person is well taken care of or assist them with the necessary tools to be successful. Rhonda also enjoys working and assisting children with medical needs.

Elise B. Gordon is a native of Washington DC where she was raised with strong family values and love. She is the proud wife of Pastor Shelton Gordon, whom she serves in ministry with at Better is the End Ministries, located in Capitol Heights, MD. Elise has a great passion to teach and help develop young minds. In August 2004, Elise launched her first business Open Vessel Family Child Care to enhance a Christian foundation in small children. Elise serves as a wife, mother, teacher, minister, and most importantly a believer of Jesus Christ.

Leslie Foxx is a native of Washington, DC and currently resides in Capitol Heights, MD. Leslie rededicated her life to Christ in February 2014. She is mother of seven beautiful and talented children, and the wife to a wonderful husband, Maurice Foxx. Leslie is grateful to God for her family, because they encourage her to hold onto the promises of God and not give up. Leslie is thankful that God has truly showed up in her and her family's lives and for His many blessings that He has poured into their spirits.

Taneya Pair is a native of Washington DC and an active member of First Baptist Church of Highland Park in Landover, MD. She is currently active in Women's Discipleship as a co-facilitator and various other ministries. With a passion for serving, a heart for supporting and guiding people with overcoming life challenges, Taneya pursued and completed her studies within Clinical Mental Health Counseling from Trinity Washington University in January 2016.

Desiree G. Smith is a native from Martinsville/Henry County, VA and currently resides in Landover, MD. She has been a soldier in army of Lord since she was a young child. She is a mother, daughter, sister, aunt, and friend. She earned a Master's Degree in Public Administration from Southeastern University in Washington, DC and holds a Bachelor's Degree in Criminal Justice from Saint Paul's College in Lawrenceville, VA.

Shanice L. Stewart is a native of Capitol Heights, MD and currently resides in Waldorf, MD with her husband, Milton and their two daughters, Melody and Destiny. Shanice earned a Bachelor's of Arts Degree in English from Coppin State University in Baltimore, MD. Shanice has a great passion to push people into their God given purpose. She encourages people to walk into their purpose and not away from it. Shanice is the author of, "Purposeless to Purposeful" and also the visionary of *Share Your Testimony*, which is a women's ministry to encourage, inspire, and strengthen women through the testimonies of other women.

Thank you so much for your love and support!

We pray that this book was a blessing to you!

Share Your
TESTIMONY